Praise for *Six Months to Live*

"Without Medjugorje, I would not have portrayed Jesus in *The Passion of the Christ*. After visiting this remote village, for the first time in my life I realized that Jesus saw me, was concerned about me, and loved me. I felt the most extraordinary sense of peace that I wished everyone could experience. When I read this book, I was struck again with this simple but life-changing truth. One of the most important lessons Artie beautifully communicates as you follow his healing journey is the need for men to be intimately involved in the spiritual leadership of their families. His words and story of an impossible healing will not only stay with you for a very long time, but challenge you to the person God called you to be." — Jim Caviezel, star, *The Passion of the Christ*

"A chance conversation in a hockey rink leads to a life-changing experience for Artie and his friends. Having known the Boyle family for many years I am certain that his story will be an inspiration to anyone who reads this book."—Bobby Orr, NHL Hall of Fame member, author of *Orr: My Story*

"In a day when mankind relies heavily on technology to provide for his needs, Artie Boyle had no choice but to rely on his faith. Stricken with terminal cancer and out of medical options, this father of thirteen traveled to a distant land to ask for a miracle. And, against all odds, he came home healed. Artie's remarkable and miraculous journey will warm your heart and rekindle your faith."—Jack Sacco, award-winning author of *Where the Birds Never Sing* and *Above the Treetops*

"Men more comfortable on a golf course, hockey rink, or in boardrooms travel to a place where they are captivated by the spiritual, and return home very different men. An engrossing memoir."—Glen Sather, President and General Manager, the New York Rangers

"Mr. Boyle's inspirational story of physical healing and spiritual transformation is one of many examples of the rich spiritual, psychological and physical fruits of Medjugorje. It reassures us of Mary's unconditional love and desire to intercede for her children."—Father Johann Roten, SM, Director of Research, Art and Special Projects, International Marian Research Institute/The Marian Library

"The wonder of the Arthur Boyle story is that it is still unfolding. A process of faith, prayer and sacraments, wrapped in the love of family and friends, and graced by the Virgin of Medjugorje, opened a healing path which continues to inspire Christian joy, hope and vision in hungry souls from the town of Hingham to

distant lands. Long may its ripple effect continue!"—
Father Simon Cadwallader, Missionary Society of St.
James the Apostle

"Artie Boyle tells us how faith, family and friends helped
him experience a miracle. Inspiring and unforgettable. A
must read!"—Bill Brett, former director of photography,
the *Boston Globe*

"My father's healing experience has been an
inspiration to me and to my eleven siblings. It changed
all of us forever. We are incredibly grateful to Jesus
and Mary for the last fourteen years with him, and the
things we have been able to share as a family. I hope
readers will be uplifted by this story of faith, family
and friends."—Brian Boyle, player, New York Rangers

Six Months to Live

Six Months to Live

Three Guys on the Ultimate Quest for a Miracle

by
Arthur P. Boyle
with
Eileen McAvoy Boylen

A Crossroad Book
The Crossroad Publishing Company
New York

The Crossroad Publishing Company
www.crossroadpublishing.com

This printing, 2015.

Printed in 2014 © 2014 by Arthur P. Boyle
Crossroad, Herder & Herder, and the crossed C logo/colophon are registered trademarks of The Crossroad Publishing Company

In continuation of our 200-year tradition of independent publishing, The Crossroad Publishing Company proudly offers a variety of books with strong, original voices and diverse perspectives. The viewpoints expressed in our books are not necessarily those of The Crossroad Publishing Company, any of its imprints or of its employees. No claims are made or responsibility assumed for any health or other benefits.

Library of Congress Cataloging-in-Publication Data available from the Library of Congress.

ISBN 978-0-8245-2020-5 (alk. paper)

Cover design by: Ray Lundgren

Book design by: Web Fusion

Photo credits: Arthur P. Boyle

Books published by The Crossroad Publishing Company may be purchased at special quantity discount rates for classes and institutional use. For information, please email info@crossroadpublishing.com.

Printed in The United States of America

FSC
www.fsc.org
MIX
Paper from responsible sources
FSC® C005010

There are many people to whom I could dedicate this book: my wife, my children, my parents, my friends that stepped out in faith to help save me. However, I feel that my greatest advocate is Our Lady. The Mother of God took me under her mantle and helped guide me to Medjugorje, where I discovered my true spirituality. I will always love Our Blessed Mother for pointing me to her loving son Jesus, and I will be forever grateful for that gift.

Our Lady Queen of Peace, pray for us.

Table of Contents

Foreword

Mary, the mother of Jesus, is a model of perfect love and obedience to her divine son. Prophesied in the Old Testament by Isaiah and Micah, in the New Testament she was first venerated by the angel Gabriel when he greeted her with the words: "Hail full of grace." And at the visitation, Elizabeth, Mary's cousin spontaneously exclaimed, "Blessed art thou among women, and blessed is the fruit of thy womb"—that is, Jesus. As Elizabeth said, Mary was chosen above all women to give birth to Jesus, and she was also granted the grace to be part of God's plan for our salvation. Jesus gave her to all of us on the cross when he said to his disciple John, "Son behold thy mother." She is mother of all, ready to help and encourage us on our faith journey.

We do not pray to Mary as if she were God or see her as our mediator. Jesus is the only mediator between us and God. Rather than worship her, we venerate her for her closeness to Jesus, and ask for her intercession, just as we would ask for prayers from a close friend.

Mary herself cannot perform miracles. Like the saints, she is a creature not a deity. She always points us to her son. At Cana, she asked Jesus to perform his first public miracle, but instructed the servants, as she instructs us, "Whatever he saith unto you, do it." (Jn. 2:5) We turn to our mother in all our needs knowing that like any mother, she wants to aid us. And how could a son ignore the pleas of his mother on our behalf? Mary and Joseph are the two human beings whom we know that Jesus honored and continues to honor, since it is a divine commandment to honor one's father and mother.

Throughout the centuries, Our Lady has appeared in various locations around the world sharing her message of love. She encourages prayer, penance and conversion and beseeches us to follow Jesus. Although the church has not approved Medjugorje as one of these Marian apparition sites, many people, like Artie Boyle, have gone there to ask for Mary's assistance. His inspirational testimony of her intercession, and his call to give witness to her motherly love, inspire us to entrust her with all our needs. Through her prayers, God lifts Mr. Boyle from great despair and carries him to the top of the mountain where he and his companions experience an intense spiritual transformation at the foot of the Cross.

From the very beginning, Our Lady has directed us to Jesus and inspired a deeper relationship with him. Through her influence, Artie learns that forgiveness, and total surrender to God's will, open the pathway for his healing. And God restores the health of Artie's body and his soul. The Blessed Mother, trusting in her son's wisdom and love for us, has always been willing to approach him on our behalf. As alive today as she has been throughout time, she takes us under her protective mantle and asks us to open our hearts to prayer. Only through prayer will we find peace and the way to salvation; through prayer we can share in the Kingdom of God.

I do hope that the book will open more people to welcoming the grace God wants to lavish on us through the intercession of Mary, our mother.

Fr. François Rossier, S.M.
Executive Director
Marian Library/International Marian Research
Institute
University of Dayton

Preface

"Now faith is the substance of things hoped for, the evidence of things not seen." (Heb. 11: 1)

The media coverage started two months after my miracle. Soon we had cameras in our home, news trucks following us to church, and many requests for interviews. In the first few years, my story was featured on three national TV shows: *The Early Show with Bryant Gumbel*, *Good Morning America*, and *20/20* as well as segments on local stations. It was the subject of many newspaper and magazine pieces including *The Boston Globe* and *The Boston Herald*. And I was a guest of Catholic Radio, and other regional shows.

The miracle occurred in Medjugorje, a tiny little town in the former Yugoslavia. I can't make anyone believe my story and I'm not offended if they don't. I can only relate the events as they happened to me, and to my two fellow travelers, Kevin Gill and Rob Griffin. But here are the medical facts. In August of 2000, I was diagnosed with an incurable condition called metastatic pulmonary renal cell carcinoma. Simply translated, it is kidney cancer that has spread to the lungs and has, or most definitely will, spread to other areas of the body. It is a Stage Four, endgame cancer.

I could survive with one kidney, and had for nine months. I would soon lose all or part of a lung, but I could probably function. However, once the disease traveled to the brain—a common progression—or to other organs without duplicates, I was done. You see, renal cell carcinoma does not respond to chemotherapy or radiation, and the only solution is to keep cutting.

No doctor can give you an exact prediction of the time you have left. They don't know. What they will share is the statistics; with my progression of the disease, I had less than a 5 percent chance of survival, with a *median* life expectancy of ten months. Renal cell carcinoma was definitely going to kill me. That was the truth, which I knew from hearing the facts:

- The fifteen-year survival rate for this stage and progression of the disease is ZERO (Laboratory for Quantitative Medicine, James Michaelson, PhD, Massachusetts General Hospital).

- Patients diagnosed with stage IV renal cell carcinoma have a median life expectancy of ten months (Oxford Journals, *Annals of Oncology*, Volume 15, Issue 4; American Urological Association).

- The chance of spontaneous remission is between 1-2 percent (Dr. Francis McGovern, MD, urologist, Massachusetts General Hospital).

I'm still alive to write this book. I left Boston for Medjugorje on September 4, 2000, with a large nodule in my upper right lung, and two smaller nodules in my lower right lung. When I returned a week later, I had a new Computed Tomography (CT) scan. The large nodule had disappeared completely, and the smaller nodules in my lower lung had shrunk to an insignificant size. My doctor at Massachusetts General Hospital, Frank McGovern, cannot explain this. He said on *The Early Show* in 2000 that "Absent a miracle, [such a] cancer will return." It hasn't. I'm still cancer-free as this book goes to press. Is this a miracle? I am sure it is. But it is up to the reader to decide for himself.

The Boyle Family.
Back Row:
Allan and Jennifer (Boyle) Pichay, Brendan, Artie Jr., Nicholas, Brian, Timothy, Christopher, Andrew.
Third Row: Gabrielle, Brianna, Judy, Artie, Kathryn, Julianne, Michelle (Boyle) Larnard and Eric Larnard.
Second Row: Gabrial, Brayden, Maria, Trevor, Michael, Gavin, Annabelle.
First Row: Shamus, Christopher, Sofia, Jacob, Christian.
Seated: Connor (Larnard), Daniel (Pichay).

Prologue

I see my children at my funeral. Twelve beautiful faces side-by-side in the front pew of Resurrection Church. These are my living children. My eighth child, Joseph Anthony, entered heaven as an infant and if I get to heaven myself, he'll be waiting for me there. How I've missed holding that soft little hand in mine and cradling him close to my heart, although, like my other twelve, he's never left my heart in all these years. Beside the children sits my lovely wife of twenty-six years, Judy, my first and only love. We've been together since I was thirteen and she was twelve. Despite my death, I know she is still a woman of great faith. But I can't bear the thought of her raising our young family alone. Who will teach them to throw a ball? Who will wipe their tears when they fall, or when life disappoints them? Who but my wife will remember them taking their first breath? Their first step?

Our shared history is now gone; the family we so lovingly created and nurtured is changed forever. I can see the two stained glass windows on either side of the altar, one of St. Michael the Archangel and the other of St. Gabriel the Archangel. Ironic. My earliest memories of the Bible came from a picture of the two sides of angels fighting—the faithful ones staying in heaven and the others falling to hell. Had I known I was going to die at forty-five, I would have spent more time here with the angels in our church. By now the pallbearers have reached the midpoint of the center aisle. The priest approaches the casket where my body lies, anoints it, and prepares me for my burial Mass. My corpse patiently waits.

Isee it all so clearly as I begin the long overnight flight. While I try to block these images, my doctors have offered little encouragement, and I know my friends worry that I might not survive the trip. This is my second bout with cancer in less than a year. As an athlete with a discipline for training and faith in my body's ability to heal, I really believed we could beat it the first time. And we did. But, now I feel like I've been handed a death sentence. I've lost a lot of weight, I'm tired, and I'm depressed. My skin is the color of a metal fork.

I remind myself that this trip is no vacation. It is supposed to be a pilgrimage. So as my traveling companions sleep from sheer exhaustion, I snap on the overhead light and start my reading. I have a King James bible, a gift from Lloyd, our airport limo driver. A self-described "non-practicing Jew," Lloyd had received it as a tip from a passenger and despite his boss's repeated requests to remove it from the car, he still had it. Our enthusiasm for the trip must have been obvious because when we arrived at Logan, he handed it to me saying, "This was meant for you." Between the bible and the books I've brought that tell the history of our destination, I will be awake all night.

It is Labor Day weekend 2000, and we are traveling to a place called Medjugorje, a tiny village nestled in the hills of Bosnia-Herzegovina, the former Yugoslavia. Until last week, I'd never heard of it. Well,

I didn't think I had. My wife says she's been telling me about it for years, but I was probably watching sports and not paying attention. My brother-in-law, Kevin Gill, and my neighbor, Rob Griffin, had learned of the miraculous apparitions of the Blessed Virgin Mary that were reported at Medjugorje—and, more importantly for me—of inexplicable healings that blessed sick pilgrims.

So here we were, Kevin, Rob, and I, hoping for a miracle of our own. Our trip came about as a result of chance conversations in hockey rinks, locker rooms and golf courses where my own dire situation broke down barriers, and led us to talk about the kind of things men generally hold deep within.

None of us would describe ourselves as deeply "spiritual." We were "guys." Our parents were devout Catholics and had done everything possible to plant the same faith in us. But other things like family, work, and the business of "life," smothered those mustard seeds. Our faith just wasn't the priority it had been for our parents. In fact, we'd never really considered why we were Catholic; just accepted it as what we were. We attended church with our wives and children on Sundays, and believed this made us "good" Catholic men, but we gave God little thought or time.

People who knew "The Boyles" from church would probably describe us as "active" parishioners, but I generally volunteered my time out of a sense of obligation rather than zeal—as something I should do because of the kids. I suspect it's the same with many men. Simply put, Rob, Kevin and I were neither heathens nor choir boys, just three guys desperate enough to take a leap of faith.

A few weeks ago, I had been diagnosed with a recurrence of renal cell carcinoma, which had now spread to my lung. Following my first diagnosis last year, I had what they call a radical nephrectomy: I was virtually cut in half, right across the middle, to have my kidney removed because of a large malignant mass. At the time, the doctors said that the growth was "contained," that they had gotten it all and I would be fine. But eight months later, they told me it was back, and that it had metastasized. As one doctor said: "The cancer could be anywhere."

My family was devastated, and while I tried to keep a brave face for them, I had never been so terrified in my life. I was exhausted from just pretending. The doctors told me starkly that there was no effective treatment. The only option was surgical extraction. And it's very risky.

On September 14, I am scheduled to have my lung removed by a thoracic surgeon at Massachusetts General Hospital. He will saw through my ribs, deflate and remove the lung, hold it in his hands, remove the tumors, and feel around to make sure he's extracted all the cancer. I may lose a piece of my lung. I may lose the whole thing. And even if this nasty little procedure "succeeds," it's just a matter of time before the malignant cells appear somewhere else. The doctors tell me the odds of survival are less than five percent. As in blackjack in Vegas, you may win a few hands, but the decks are stacked against you. The disease, like the house, always wins.

I am going to Medjugorje to be healed and to be with the Blessed Mother. I'm hoping for a miracle. And, although I might not actually see her, I feel strongly that she will touch me in some way. It's the only hope I have.

Judy and Artie Boyle, February 9, 1974.

1

Teenage Newlyweds

We started our married life with no jobs, no college degrees, and very little money. Yet, we were happy. And the people who said we would fail were dead wrong.

1

On December 29, 1973, I celebrated my nineteenth birthday. Six weeks later I was married. Judy Foley was eighteen, my first girlfriend—and luckily for me, the love of my life. I was thirteen when I fell in love with her (she was twelve), and we have been together ever since.

Judy was shagging baseballs for her dad at a little league tryout and when he picked me for his team, I'm sure he wasn't picturing a potential son-in-law! As she tells the story, I became her first boyfriend, and her dad's worst nightmare. Her father had very strong feelings about her "dating" at such an early age and he made no bones about it. From the very beginning, there was much conflict over our young love.

But our wedding day proved to be beautiful. There had been a blizzard the day before and everything was covered with fresh white snow, the "first day" kind that sticks to the tree branches and covers the streets and sidewalks. It was a large wedding with 225 guests at Our Lady of Good Counsel Church on Sea Street in Quincy, Massachusetts, where Judy had made all her sacraments, followed by a reception at the Sons of Italy. Most of the wedding party was too young to drink the wedding toast and many of the guests were too.

Judy was absolutely radiant. She was, and is, a gorgeous woman; and that day she wore a borrowed gown and the hairstyle most popular at proms that year, banana curls. We weren't far past proms ourselves. We had a car—well...Judy had a car, but this was an unusual time in American history. An oil embargo had created a major gasoline shortage. So, instead of driving off into the sunset with "just married" on the rear window, we relied on trains, buses, and taxis for our honeymoon in the Poconos.

Judy was at peace about our marriage because we had been together so long, and she took the sacrament very seriously. She understood her new responsibilities and had a good idea how her life was about to change.

I didn't. I knew I loved her. I'd never loved anyone else. But I also remember thinking how great it was to be getting out of my parents' house.

We started our married life with no jobs, no college degrees, and very little money. Yet, we were happy. And the people who said we would fail were dead wrong.

Judy was clearly the adult in the relationship. She had been working at Friendly's Ice Cream and managing her own money since she was sixteen. I was definitely not mature enough to be married, and certainly not ready to become a father. But we both got jobs. I worked nights so Judy could be home during the day and we shared one car for transportation.

She found us a small apartment with trendy shag carpeting and brand new appliances, making her the envy of all her friends. When my mother suggested we live in the projects in Germantown for $60 a month, Judy was horrified. I had begun my life in Boston's Columbia Point public housing and couldn't see the down side. But Judy prevailed and we set up housekeeping on West Street in Quincy.

Jen was born later that year and we became a family. Judy and I were both ecstatic, but we had so little money that when friends came to visit, they often brought a gallon of milk instead of a bottle of wine. People were very generous. Once someone anonymously left a $20 bill in our mailbox, and we were thrilled because it nearly covered our weekly grocery bill.

Judy's mother had had eight children and taught her to keep house at an early age. So, she soon eradicated my slovenly ways. I learned to clean, change diapers, heat bottles, and do laundry, and when her father came to the door one day finding me with a baby in one arm and a vacuum cleaner in the other, he asked Judy, "What have you *done* to him?"

We decided then—although in hindsight it might have been more at Judy's direction—to be open to as many children as God wanted to give us. However, we underestimated his generosity and never expected to be entrusted with thirteen perfect little souls!

We had three children in three years. Our first son was born the year after Jen and we named him Artie, Jr. I was thrilled to have a boy. I had given up college hockey for marriage and hoped that one of my children could someday live out my dream of competing for an NCAA championship. Confident the baby would have Jen's intelligence and our combined athletic ability (Judy was a track star, gymnast and cheerleader in high school), I couldn't wait to see him excel in competitive sports. But that wasn't to be.

Little Artie walked and talked later than Jen and his younger sister, Michelle, (born the following year), and we started noticing unusual behavior when he was about eighteen months. He wasn't making eye contact, he started withdrawing, and did odd things like biting blocks or leaving the room when we were talking to him. Sandwiched between Jen and Michelle who were both very bright and verbal, his actions really stood out.

Judy was studying early childhood education at a local college and knew something was wrong. I simply refused to see it. She took him to Children's Hospital in Boston for tests, and it became apparent that he had major cognitive issues. They diagnosed him with autism. When the doctor used the word "retarded," a commonly accepted term then, I wanted to punch him in the face. We learned that Artie would not live the life we had imagined. In fact, he would struggle with the smallest of daily tasks.

I had no training for this. What was I supposed to do with him? My first, and at the time, only son. I was distraught. And very, *very*, angry. We laid awake nights wondering what would happen to him. Would he ever graduate from high school? Hold a job? Get married? We finally had to accept that we were the parents of an autistic child. This was extremely difficult. Back then we could never have anticipated the joy that he would bring to us and to the rest of the family. And he still does to this day.

We made sure that Artie, Jr., participated in as many activities as possible. He learned to swim. He played hockey on a special needs team I coached. When the family went skiing, I would tie a rope around his waist so he could go down the mountain laughing in front of me. He loved it.

When Artie turned eighteen, his two closest siblings were going to college and he wanted to go, too. He couldn't, of course. But we wanted to send him somewhere he could continue his education and learn to live independently. One of the hardest things we have ever done is to let Artie enroll at Cardinal Cushing School in Hanover, Massachusetts. This residential program for students with various mental and behavioral challenges allowed him to live outside our sheltered home for the first time, and helped him transition to an "after twenty-two" adult group home. Today he lives with his roommate, Lionel, in his own apartment. Artie, Jr., works during the day and one of us, or his siblings, stays with them at night. He's very proud of his independence and we are, too.

Our eighth child, Joseph Anthony, was born on October 1, 1986. A seemingly happy and healthy baby, he wouldn't live to see his first birthday. When he was just eight weeks old, Judy went to his crib one morning and found him unresponsive. I don't think I have ever heard a scream like hers that morning. It was primal, otherworldly—pain, horror, anguish and fear, all rolled into one heartbreaking sound. "Call 911!" she cried out as I ran from the second floor. Our school aged children were lined up on the stairs, watching as I desperately tried to revive their new baby brother. The ambulance arrived in minutes, but at the hospital the doctors told us Joseph had been gone before we found him and that there was nothing anyone could have done. I will never forget the cold November day that Judy cradled his small white casket in her lap from the funeral home to St. Paul's cemetery.

It was one of the lowest moments of our lives. We struggled with it individually and as a family for many years. To some degree we still do, and probably always will. Not long after his death, we sold our house and moved so we wouldn't be reminded of that terrible day every time we passed his room.

The pain of losing Joseph was unimaginable, and the kids were severely traumatized. Judy, as always, turned to prayer. I turned to hockey and other sports. She wanted to talk, to go to support groups. I didn't. Finally one day, feeling alone in her grief, she actually sat on top of me, grabbed me by the chin, and said I had to open up and talk about our loss. You can't be subtle with me. It often takes a strong physical stimulus to get my attention. For years it seemed Judy and I were on the same team but playing under completely different coaches.

You see, I didn't have her faith. I was, for lack of a better description, a "convenience Catholic." Yes, I believed in God, and I went to church because I thought it made me a good person and a good father. I believed that without religion there would be complete social anarchy. But I rarely thought about God. People who knew me then might say, "Well, weren't you involved in CCD and Pre-Cana, and other parish programs?" I was. However, that had been Judy's wish and something I'd felt we should do as a couple. I never really thought about it. I am ashamed to say I had no personal relationship with God and drew no real strength or comfort from his presence.

People often wonder why we chose to have thirteen children. Some of them even wonder this aloud to us! But we feel blessed by each of them. Judy will look at our youngest and say "What did we ever do without Andrew? How did we ever get along without him?" She feels the same way about each of them. And I do too.

After Artie Jr.'s diagnosis, and then Joseph's death, many people thought we shouldn't have any more. And watching the pain we endured then, I'm sure that advice was well-intended. Even Judy's faith was tested, and there were many tears, sleepless nights, and great anger about what had happened to us and to our family. We kept asking each other, "Why?" But there were no answers.

In fact, for a year Judy thought to herself, "Okay, God. I've said 'yes' to you all these years. I've done everything you've asked of me. From here on in, you're on your own. I'm not helping anymore." She says it was reading the Book of Job that opened her eyes. Job was a man who felt betrayed by God and was angry that he hadn't protected him, who thought he knew better than God. But God replies to Job in Chapter 38, "Where were you when I founded the earth? Tell me, if you have understanding. Who determined its size; do you know? Who stretched out the measuring line for it? Into what were its pedestals sunk, and who lay the cornerstone while the morning stars sang in chorus?" He reminds Job who hung those stars, who created the sea, who commanded the morning and showed dawn its place. From meditating on this story, Judy finally came to see that God needed nothing from her. Quite the opposite. She would never understand why he took Joseph. But he was still God. And she was still just Judy.

Faith sustains you in both the best and worst of times, but it doesn't spare you. Even Jesus wept at the death of his friend, Lazarus. We each will have reasons to weep. Ultimately, Judy's trust in a loving God helped us to heal and move forward. She still believed that when God provides children, he doesn't leave you alone to care for them. He follows up.

We didn't keep having children because we expected them all to be perfect. In fact, none of them is perfect. We didn't know that one of our children would become a doctor, or that another would be a first-round NHL draft pick, any more than we knew one would have autism and another would die in his crib. We kept having children because we loved them, and they were the glue that held the family together. We wanted to be happy, and despite the challenges, we were.

People who knew us at our seven-bedroom home on Olmsted Drive might be very surprised by our humble beginnings in that little apartment on West Street. We had our first five children in relative poverty before we could afford our first tiny two-bedroom house across from our former junior high. Twenty-one years, eleven children, and seven moves later, we arrived at the Hingham home where this journey began.

Brian and Artie Boyle.

2

Something's Not Right

*Although I didn't know it, this was the beginning of a
journey that would change all of our lives forever.*

In September 1999, we were just an average American family living in the suburbs of Boston. Well—average for a family of thirteen children, with seven still living at home, and three away at college. Unlike us, most people don't pay for diapers and college tuitions simultaneously; our parenting and financial responsibilities were enormous. Life was chaotic in the Boyle household, but my wife and I thrived on it, and worked hard to carve out solo time for each of the children. It's not easy being one of thirteen, so we knew that individual attention was very important.

Judy is a master of organization, with her color-coded charts and calendars in our mudroom, and she manages the family like a well-oiled machine. There are file folders for each of the children containing all their school records, schedules, and other vital information. We have occasionally forgotten to pick someone up from school or activities, but for the most part the system has worked as planned.

First-time visitors to our home sometimes ask if we are moving houses, because every surface is clean and there's not a thing out of place. We actually have moved a lot—Judy gets the bug every three years or so—but she's such a meticulous housekeeper that things always look perfect. My wife firmly believes that God controls our lives, but she controls our environment. And if everyone left his or her belongings around the house, with all the hockey sticks, pads, soccer balls, and dirty uniforms, it would look like one big locker room. Even out of those uniforms, our children, by necessity, have learned to work as a team and we have been thrilled to see them become best friends.

Most of them were born here in Hingham, a coastal community fifteen miles southeast of Boston. Its downtown harbor area is lined with buildings dating back to the Revolutionary War, and on its perimeter stand the stately homes of sea captains who flourished in America's early maritime economy. We have lived at six different addresses since we arrived in 1982, and our children consider this town "home."

For the most part, life here was good. Somehow, in between the kids' school and recreational activities, I still managed to play sports and enjoy the company of my wife of twenty-five years. My primary goal was to be a good husband and father, and for the most part, I thought I was. Then everything changed.

In August 1999 I was on the fourth hole at Hatherly Country Club in Scituate, a neighboring town, when I first experienced the burning sensation. It felt like I had swallowed a flame. The heat started from deep inside, emanating through my entire body. I had never experienced anything like it in my life. Although I had felt my usual energy at the outset, I was now suddenly too fatigued to continue. As a good golfer with a competitive nature and passion for the sport, I had never quit before the eighteenth hole. But now I just couldn't go on.

A few weeks later, at the beginning of a new hockey season, I drove to the rink but never got beyond the locker room because I was suddenly too exhausted to play. In fact, the very idea of putting on skates was overwhelming. The opening game was always exhilarating for me but that day I felt like I was slogging in wet cement. Why? I just couldn't understand it. I was only forty-four years old and had always been in perfect health. Or so I thought.

The burning feeling on the golf course was new, but I started to remember how tired I had been at our daughter Jen's wedding the previous month. It was a destination wedding at Disneyworld and we were all thrilled to be there. Jen is our oldest child and was the second to marry. The wedding itself was a big deal, not to mention the kids' excitement about the setting. But I was constantly fatigued. The days would start well but I would go downhill quickly, and my eagerness to visit Epcot or one of the other theme parks drained away. I dragged myself there for the kids, but had to stop and rest often. At night I faded fast and I didn't even want to dance at the wedding reception. This was not like me. I didn't know what was wrong at the time, so I attributed my weariness to Florida's summer heat, to travel, and to lack of sleep.

By September, I knew it was something more. When our daughter, Michelle, showed us pictures from our granddaughter's christening, I barely recognized myself. My face was drawn, my skin color, ashen; and

I was losing weight. A lot of weight. Something was clearly not right. I hated doctors and hadn't been to see one in thirty years, but seeing those photos scared the life out of me. Judy insisted I have a complete physical, and for once I agreed. Although I didn't know it, we were beginning a journey that would change all of our lives forever.

Christmas, 1999—just after Artie's first diagnosis of renal cell carcinoma.
Left to right: Matt Watkins, Kevin Gill, Artie Boyle, Bob Torraco, Artie Boyle, Jr.

3

Tested

Had we listened to that doctor, I believe I'd be dead today.

In September 1999, Judy made an appointment for me at a local health center. I didn't have a primary care doctor, so this was the quickest way to be seen. Like many other suburban clinics, it sat in a simple brick building with a parking lot tucked behind a shopping plaza. The waiting room was filled with coughing kids and adults with ailments ranging from sprained ankles to nasty stomach viruses—all well within the capabilities of this type of practice. Many of the doctors on duty are affiliated with major Boston hospitals, but the facilities themselves aren't designed to address serious illness.

Seeing a forty-four-year-old athletic man with no family history of cancer, the doctors weren't looking for it. On the contrary, the physician thought I might have Lyme disease or some other kind of infection. Not good, but nothing requiring surgery or hospitalization. The woman had never seen me before and I had no medical records for comparison, so to her I might have looked okay.

She ordered blood work, which revealed anemia—a red flag because it's very unusual in men. So she referred me to a specialist at a local hospital who ran more tests before diagnosing Barrett's esophagus, an irritation of the tube leading from the mouth to the stomach. He prescribed an antacid and told me to return in a month.

As we left, Judy told me she lacked confidence in this doctor because he had a "golf picture" on the wall. Since I've been known to frequent the links myself, I laughed and told her not to worry. Maybe her intuition was kicking in, but I remember being relieved that nothing was seriously wrong, and expected to feel better soon.

That didn't happen. In fact, my weight continued to plummet until I'd lost forty-five pounds. When my symptoms persisted, I returned to the hospital for the scheduled follow-up visit. The physician reassured me the drug hadn't taken effect yet and that I should continue it for another month. Even with my limited medical knowledge, this didn't make sense to me. Judy may have been off about the golf, but she was right about the doctor. Had we listened to him, I believe I would be dead today.

I was feeling worse and started having severe night sweats, so bad that I was soaking through the sheets. I told Jen, who was a second-year medical student at the time, and she was very concerned because this is often indicative of cancer. As ridiculous as it seems now, we had wasted the entire month of October waiting for an antacid to work magic. We didn't know where to turn for help. I felt like I was running out of time and hoped it wasn't already too late. But this is where miracles began to happen and God started to take over our lives.

Boston has some of the finest hospitals in the world and people come from around the globe seeking medical care. Massachusetts General (MGH), the oldest and largest such facility in Boston, is a teaching hospital for

Harvard Medical School and is consistently rated one of the best in the country. This is where we wanted to go, but we had no idea how to navigate the process. Our "house specialties" were obstetrics and pediatrics, neither of which was going to help here.

Jen had suggested a CT scan but we couldn't get an appointment with anyone at MGH for a month. Judy placed several calls but very few doctors were accepting new patients, and those that were had long waiting lists. We had already wasted so much time treating the wrong symptoms that we felt we couldn't delay.

Then out of the blue a very good friend from Vermont showed up at our back door one day. David just happened to be in the area, hundreds of miles from home. So Judy invited him to stay for a cup of tea and told him about my problem. On hearing this, David reminded Judy that his sister was a nurse at Mass General. She led us to Dr. Richard Pingree, a clinic physician.

So we drove to MGH, a city-like complex of more than twenty different buildings at the foot of Beacon Hill, with taxis, cars, ambulances, wheelchairs, pedestrians, and medical staff coming and going at all hours. All the international visitors and doctors make the place look like the United Nations. For someone as averse to doctors as I was, this was extremely overwhelming and I felt I was being sucked into a vortex of medical mayhem.

I was there to see Dr. Pingree, a primary care doctor who could get us "into the system" and refer me to a specialist. A middle-aged man with blue eyes, he was a very, very busy clinician with at least forty people sitting in the waiting room. As soon as someone would leave, another patient would step up to take his place. Clearly in a hurry, Dr. Pingree heard my story and ordered more blood tests. When I returned a few days later, he told me I was even more anemic than in September. He referred me to a hematologist, Dr. Leonard Ellman. Ellman was a nice guy, more of a scientist than a conversationalist, but even without words, I knew he was concerned. Like each doctor before him, he took some blood and ordered some X–rays, which revealed nothing new. He agreed to the CT scan Jen had recommended, scheduling it at a satellite facility in Chelsea, north of the city, in the shadow of the Tobin Bridge.

The radiologist administering the test said that I was not breathing properly and that she needed to take more images. This made me still more nervous. Although she told me the results wouldn't be available until the next day, I found myself driving back across the bridge towards the hospital instead of heading home. I knew something was seriously wrong. Just as I approached the MGH exit, my cell phone rang and it was Dr. Ellman's office. His nurse calmly asked if I could come in right away.

Dr. Ellman was waiting for me at the door of his office and invited me to come in. As I sat down, he looked me in the eye and said, "You have renal cell carcinoma—cancer of the kidney." I nearly fell on the floor. In fact, it felt like I was in an elevator that had suddenly plunged fifty stories to the basement. The doctor offered me a tranquilizer, something I'm sure he dispenses like lollipops in his line of work. I declined, but could barely keep my composure. I was devastated. All I could think about was my wife and kids. How they would live without me? What would they do? Who would watch over them? How would my three little boys get through an incredibly tough life without a father? Who would do the little everyday things I'd taken for granted—like playing catch, driving them to hockey, wrestling on the lawn? Would I see my little girls grow up? In an instant my life had changed. I had just become a cancer patient.

The doctor provided more details but I barely heard them. He said I needed to see an oncologist immediately. He placed a call to a colleague, Dr. Robert Carey, and sent me on my way. All these months waiting for a diagnosis, and now they could see me the same day.

Dr. Ellman directed me to Cox-2, the cancer ward at MGH. I stumbled out of his office and down the long dark hallway to the waiting room where I sat for three hours in a daze. I could hardly see through the tears in my eyes, but when I did look up I saw people with the same problem. Cancer. That made me feel a little better. Many others had survived it. I had played sports all my life, and with my physical strength and endurance, surely I could train for this too! It seems almost laughable now. The competitive me suddenly had a new opponent. It was me versus carcinoma.

I still believed that I was in control. Even with the many unforeseen and sometimes tragic events in my life, I still didn't get it. God was simply not on my radar screen and it never occurred to me to ask him for help. I had a fist-sized tumor on my kidney; the pancreas and the spleen were inflamed; and the lymph nodes were enlarged, which meant that the cancer had likely spread. It was not a pretty picture. Even still, in those three agonizing hours, I never prayed.

I didn't know how to tell my wife. In fact, it took me a long time to muster the courage to call anyone. I finally phoned my daughter Michelle, and when I shared the news her reaction was stunned silence. I don't think she spoke more than five words. It was an abbreviated conversation because Dr. Carey called me into his office. He looked at me and said, "You just got a kick in the balls." I thought that was an apt description and I found his candor refreshing. It didn't make things any better, but at least he understood.

I asked him about treatment. There was nothing uplifting about his answers. He explained that renal cell carcinoma does not respond to traditional cancer regimens. There is no cure. Neither chemotherapy nor radiation will eradicate or even halt the progression of the disease. The only option is extraction. He said, "When in doubt, cut it out." I instantly agreed. He made a call to a urologist, Dr. Francis McGovern, who could see me that very afternoon: the worse your condition, the quicker the appointment. Not a good sign. But it was already 5 p.m. I was exhausted and I wanted Judy to be there when I met the surgeon. Dr. McGovern agreed to see us first thing in the morning to answer our questions and schedule the surgery.

Judy was also at a doctor's appointment that afternoon. I would learn later that just as I was receiving my life-altering diagnosis, she put down her magazine in the waiting room. She was reading an article on non-Hodgkins lymphoma, and some of the symptoms—weight loss, fatigue, and anemia—were so similar that she became convinced that lymphoma was what I had. She was stunned. It was like foreshadowing. She thought it might be God's way of warning her so that she could deal with bad news later. She may have been right.

I had already spoken with Michelle and decided I couldn't wait until I got home to tell Judy. We had virtually grown up together and she was my very best friend. I had just gotten news that would dramatically change our world and I needed her to know.

I tried reaching her on her cell but the coverage in Scituate was terrible and I simply couldn't get through. I kept trying every few minutes. When I reached her half an hour later I didn't know what to say. I struggled to get the words out, "Judy, I have some bad news. The doctor said I have cancer, and it looks like it's pretty advanced." She reacted much as Michelle had. I wasn't sure if she was being silent or if the call was cutting in and out. It was probably a little bit of both. She had no words. We said we would talk when we got home, so she spent the rest of the ride home calming herself, gathering her thoughts, and figuring out what to say. I think we both needed that time and space.

The drive home seemed endless. In my mind, the traffic just went away. Cars whizzed by. I blindly passed familiar landmarks, and have no memory of going through Quincy to Weymouth to Hingham. I went from "point A" to "point B" without knowing exactly how I got there.

It was the same for Judy. We met at home, we held onto one another, and said nothing for a very long time. We are not thick-skinned people by any means. However, we had just been dealt such an unimaginable blow that neither of us knew how to react. Part of you feels like you have to be strong for the other person, while the rest of you is sure that if you let down your guard even a little bit, you'll completely fall apart. Judy had always been stoic for her family and was saving the worst of her emotions for when she could experience them alone. That evening, I remember both of us being very solemn, trying to figure out what to do—not that there were any good options on the table—and mentally preparing for the appointment the next day.

I saw myself sick and miserable, painting all kinds of unpleasant pictures in my mind without any idea of their reality. Judy was doing the same thing. Even for her, prayer would come later. Not yet. Not that night.

We had definitely been tested as a couple and as a family in the past, but nothing prepares you for this. The tears and waves of emotion hadn't set in yet. That would come later. While we would trudge through all the stages of grief in the coming months, this afternoon the prevailing mood was shock. The news was unfathomable and I'm not sure it really sunk in. Zombie-like, we walked through the usual routine for the kids, ridden with angst about our meeting the next morning. As the evening wore on, Michelle came over. Jen came later. Neither had much to say but just having them there was a great comfort. Sometimes a person's presence is simply a blessing.

The next day we held hands in the doctor's office. Dr. McGovern was pragmatic and clinical in his description of the procedure. It would take two surgeons. He would perform the urological surgery and then a gastroenterologist would excise the affected part of the pancreas. Dr. McGovern was honest. He explained that while the kidney operation would be painful and invasive, pancreatic cancer surgery is one of the most difficult operations a surgeon can perform. It's also one of the most grueling for patients. The incision would bleed through the wound, there are often other complications, and the recovery is lengthy.

McGovern made no promises about the outcome. But my odds of long-term survival were significantly better if the cancer was contained in my kidney. If it had spread to the pancreas or the lymph nodes, as he said he suspected, we were just buying time. Judy was so stunned she couldn't utter a word.

She would later tell me that in true biblical tradition she had been rebuking the illness the whole time. Just as Jesus rebuked the sickness of the family member in the house of Simon (Lk 4:38-44) Judy believes we can take charge over illness and order it to leave.

This procedure would be an ugly exercise and the prognosis was not good, but I was determined to live. He scheduled me for December 9, only twenty-one days away.

The late Fr. Ed McDonough praying with two women.

4

Prayer Warriors

As I was praying, something physical struck me in the chest. It came rushing into me, startled me, and knocked me backwards. I looked at my wife and said, "What was that?" Puzzled, she asked, "What was what?"

have said that I was determined to live. And I was. But the idea of a gruesome operation with questionable results nearly paralyzed me with fear. My feelings shifted by the day, and then by the hour.

I told myself I could beat cancer. Next I began contemplating death. It was hard not to. Anyone who has experienced an advanced cancer diagnosis understands the mood swings. Despite my best efforts, negative thoughts filled my head and depression overtook me.

As I lived with anguish, Judy, her family, and my parents turned to the Bible. They clung to this passage:

Is any man sick among you? Let him bring in the priests of the church, and let them pray over him, anointing him with oil in the name of the Lord.

And the prayer of faith shall save the sick man: and the Lord shall raise him up: and if he be in sins, they shall be forgiven him....For the continual prayer of a just man availeth much. (Jas 5:14-16)

My personal "prayer warriors" began storming heaven. They printed hundreds of St. Anthony prayer cards inscribed with my name, placed them in local churches, and soon perfect strangers were praying for me. Judy took me to Father Ed McDonough, a world-renowned "healing priest," at Boston's Our Lady of Perpetual Help Basilica, more commonly known as the "Mission Church."

What directed her there? I would say the Holy Spirit. Father Ed's healing gifts had been credited with countless documented healings over the years—ranging from deafness to epilepsy, comas, cancers, and a host of other illnesses.

Our Lady of Perpetual Help is a huge Romanesque building, and one of its major features is the shrine dedicated to its patroness. In a beautifully painted alcove with stained glass windows, her statue looms over an intricate marble altar with the archangels Michael and Gabriel standing watch on either side, and two urns filled with crutches and canes of the many people who had been cured there. Many of these miracles are attributed to the weekly novena to Our Lady. During World War II, the church's continuous Wednesday novenas drew an astonishing 25,000 people—more than the daily attendance at nearby Fenway Park—but novena participation has diminished dramatically since then. You might have seen this church on television because, ten years after our visit, it would host the funeral of Senator Edward M. Kennedy.

This November day in 1999, I didn't know much about either Father Ed or this place of miracles, but Judy told me I was going, and I always do what she tells me. Well, sometimes. I definitely defer to her on spiritual matters.

She picked me up at work and drove me there. I wasn't particularly optimistic about what this strange priest could do for me, but at this point I would try anything. During the ride, we listened to a radio show about Blessed Faustina, someone we'd never heard of before, but who stirred my wife's curiosity. Judy insisted that I needed a Miraculous Medal. I did not wear jewelry of *any* kind then, but to please her I said that I would get one.

When we arrived, nearly a thousand people lined the pews. I knelt and prayed as hard as I could, and for the first time in my life, I prayed with my heart. I let everything go and turned over all my pain to God. That's when I felt like I'd been hit. Something palpable came rushing into me, startling me, and knocking me backwards. I looked at my wife and said, "What was that?" Puzzled, she asked, "What was *what?*" I couldn't say.

Father moved through the crowd praying individually with whoever stepped forward. When Father placed his hands on me, warmth radiated from my waist to the top of my head. Inexplicably, my color instantly went from cancer grey back to flesh tone. I felt wonderful!

For reasons I didn't understand, Father sent us to Tom Tam, an Eastern holy man in Boston's Chinatown, a short subway ride away. I sat in a chair across from Tom, and without touching me, he moved his hands in a waving motion across my body. Oddly enough, I had the same sensation I had experienced in church. With instant energy, I bounded up the stairs out into the cold air, not having felt this good in a long time! I felt so good that on the way out the door I yelled to Tom that I was going to get my blood tested. He laughed and said that it was a good idea. (The next day, a good friend and medical doctor would administer a blood test which showed my blood numbers had returned to normal—a medical improbability.)

Father McDonough's part in my story did not end that day. He would play an unexpected role later on in my journey, one that would not unfold for nearly a year.

After driving from Boston, Judy dropped me off at work. I had some things to do at the office and said I would see her at home. When I returned to my locked car, there was a Miraculous Medal on a man's chain in the passenger seat. I called Judy and said, "That was fast. How did you do that?" She said, "Do what?" To this day we do not know how the medal got there—none of our children or family ever claimed credit—but we are very grateful for the gift, and fifteen years later I still wear that medal every day.

That same evening, Judy discovered a voicemail from someone who found the St. Anthony novenas that Judy had left in church. The voice said, "Judy, you don't know me but I have been praying for Artie. Several months ago, I lost a relic in my home. I just found it and I'd like him to have it." It was a relic of Blessed Faustina, the sister whom we had learned about that day on the way to Mission Church.

We attended many other healing Masses. We prayed with Father Tom DiLorenzo and Father Francisco

"Paco" Anzoategui, two priests widely known for their healing gifts, as well as Father James Rafferty of St. Paul's in Hingham. There was also an all-night prayer vigil for me at our parish in Hingham. My eight-year-old son's entire hockey team was there and placed their hockey shirts over the front railing at the church. I knew something wonderful was happening and I felt then that with the help of God I could beat this cancer.

But first I had to get through surgery. One common misconception about faith-based healings is that God does not work through doctors, that if one really trusts in the power of prayer, he doesn't seek professional medical care. I don't believe this, nor do any of the healing priests I visited. Without the Almighty, there would be no physicians or medical science. Sometimes healing is instantaneous and doesn't require surgeries or medications. In other cases, the surgeons are guided by the hand of Jesus, with miraculous outcomes.

Other times, for reasons only God understands, the healing does not happen the way we hope. This is one of life's mysteries that many spiritual teachers have spoken about through the ages. Based on my CT scans it was clear I needed an operation, so we went ahead.

On the morning of December 9, my dad drove me to Mass General for the eight-hour surgery. I can still remember his worried expression as they wheeled me off to the operating room. When I came out of recovery very late that evening, I heard Judy saying, "They got all the cancer!" My parents, my sister Kathleen, and my daughter Kathryn echoed Judy's words, "They got it all! They got it all!"

But, soon unbearable pain overtook me, and continued for 48 hours. The general anesthesia had cleared my system and left me writhing in misery. This shouldn't have been a surprise. The doctors had cut me in two, removed a kidney, the tumor, the adrenal gland, and some muscle and local tissue, and then stitched me back together like Frankenstein. The nurses were wonderful and did whatever they could to make me more comfortable, but the trauma to my body was undeniable and even the smallest movement cut like a knife. I vowed I'd *never* have surgery again.

However, that wasn't in the cards. While I was there, additional CT scans showed a golf ball-sized tumor on my thyroid, and the doctors feared that the cancer might have traveled from the kidney. They did a gruesome biopsy, sticking eight- or nine-inch needles into my throat while I watched on the video screen. A few months later, I would need to have half my thyroid removed.

But amidst the ordeals, there was some remarkably good news this December day. A protective membrane had grown between the pancreas and the kidney tumor, preventing the cancer from spreading. A miracle? I can't say, but I think that this protection was the outcome of what I had experienced at Mission Church.

Doctor McGovern called a few weeks later with the pathology results. He was absolutely ecstatic. The margins were clear and everything looked great. He told me I was healed and to go on with my life.

And I did. I believed I had been healed by Jesus Christ through the intercession of His Blessed Mother Mary, to whom I directed many of my prayers. I wanted to show my deep gratitude and I prayed that I would know how. I asked God what He wanted me to do. I heard nothing, so I did nothing.

The healing had changed the course of my cancer, but it apparently hadn't changed *me*. Competitive as ever, I was on the golf course six weeks later wearing sixty steri-strips. I was back! I didn't forget about God, but I lost the sense of letting go and trusting him. I was no longer abandoning myself as I had that day at Mission Church. Feeling back in control of my life, I was swept up by the responsibilities of work and my active family, and let my renewed spirituality fade into the background. And for eight months, it did—until August, when we learned the cancer was back, and that this time it would likely kill me.

If God was trying to recapture my attention, it worked. My follow-up scan results shook me to the core. Beforehand, I had viewed this test as a formality, as nothing to be concerned about. The docs were just being "careful." I was certain everything would be fine because, according to the post-surgery pathology report in January, all the margins were clear. I knew God had healed me, and couldn't imagine that I would be sick again seven months later. I was only forty-five years old! None of us can understand the ways of God; I know that. But this news stunned me.

My first inkling that something was wrong came when the radiologist complained, once again, about my breathing. I was at the same Chelsea facility with the same tech, and she was taking extra pictures. Not good. Despite her best efforts, I knew she was stalling and that something wasn't right. She wouldn't tell me anything except that the results would be available in a day or so. I was out of my skin with anxiety.

The next day I went to see my oncologist, Dr. Carey. He's a good guy who tells it like it is. When I arrived in his office, his first words were: "I'm overworked." That's not exactly what you want to hear from someone whom you're depending upon to keep you alive. The poor man looked exhausted. It went downhill from there. The scan had revealed three nodules (tumors) in my right lung. One of the nodules was growing, which led them to believe the cancer had metastasized. I was confused and scared. How could it have recurred so quickly?

This time, Dr. Carey referred me to a thoracic (lung) surgeon, Dr. Cameron Wright, and scheduled me for a visit the next day. Judy was impressed with Dr. Wright but my situation was complicated and I remember her suggesting that we consult some different doctors. I listened, but I felt as if it almost didn't matter. I knew she would handle it, so I left it to her. As usual, her instincts would prove correct. It's a pity she doesn't bet horses.

My state of mind was far worse this time around. I was profoundly depressed and not nearly as convinced that I could beat this. To be honest, I didn't think that I would. I found it difficult to concentrate when I prayed and any peace I achieved was fleeting.

On a scale of one to ten, over the years I would have rated my faith in God somewhere around the middle, maybe a "six" or so. Judy, on the other hand, goes off the charts, scoring (I'd say) a "fifteen." But no matter how deeply you believe, at times like this we all have doubts. As the father of the sick child in Mark 9: 24 said, "Lord I believe! Help my unbelief." In August 2000 we could totally identify with those words.

Some years later, a neighbor told me about meeting my wife walking through the neighborhood shortly after my second diagnosis. It was the only time she had ever seen Judy frightened. Judy kept saying, "What am I going to do? What am I going to do with all these kids?" At the time, I felt terrible at what she might have to endure. What Judy went through still brings me to tears.

Both doctors recommended a biopsy on the lung nodules. That test would confirm that I did indeed have metastatic renal cell carcinoma. The first time they said that I had cancer, I didn't think that it could be any worse. I was wrong. The disease had returned so quickly, and with such a vengeance, that I felt doomed. When the oncologist delivered the news it sounded like a death sentence.

People often ask how I went from being "struck" by God and believing he had healed me, to feeling desperate and hopeless eight months later. I guess I thought that I had disappointed him by falling away from spirituality, and maybe this was the result. Like most people, I got caught up in work, the kids, and earthly concerns and took God for granted.

Why should God help me again? In my eyes, looking at it in business terms, I was a bad investment. I still didn't get it. Judy prayed as always, saying she was "taking it to the foot of the Cross." I didn't know what she meant. I went through the motions in total despair, barely able to put one foot in front of the other.

Judy once again reenlisted the army of prayer warriors, while we hit the healing service circuit. At St. Mary's Church in Hanover, Massachusetts, Father Paco, who had prayed with me before the last surgery, conducted another prayer session. There were at least thirty family members and friends in attendance and Father encouraged them to lay hands on me as he prayed. My body began to tremble and my companions said they felt something go through the entire group. I wasn't aware of it. Despite amazing spiritual experiences I couldn't forget my doctor's words. I was almost certainly going to die.

Someone told us about a holistic medicine practitioner, who agreed to see me twice that August— which was remarkable because she was always booked months in advance. She recommended certain vitamins and herbs to strengthen my body for surgery and for post-operative healing.

My daughter Jennifer and her husband Allen, both medical students, accompanied Judy and me to the thoracic surgeon on August 22. Dr. Wright very patiently answered all of their questions. He was convinced that he needed to perform major surgery as soon as possible. He would cut through my ribs, take the lung in his hands, excise the tumors, and then palpate it to determine if he got all the cancer. Until he opened me up he wasn't going to know if he could save any part of the lung. Jennifer and Allen were satisfied with his responses and his resolve, but I began to feel differently. I don't know why, but it was in his office that I began to doubt I'd ever have this surgery. However, Dr. Wright scheduled it for September 14, just a few weeks away. Although I didn't know it at the time, this date held a greater significance—which would soon become clear.

Our fifteen-year-old son, Brian, had just been drafted by the Quebec Major Junior Hockey league, a Canadian franchise of teams that develops school-age players for the NHL. Much as they would if preparing for the Olympics, kids move to the team's city under the care of a host family as they continue their education. From the time he put on his first pair of skates, Brian had dreamed of playing professional hockey, so on the weekend before Labor Day in 2000, I took him to Canada to learn more about this opportunity.

I now doubted that I would live to see him achieve his goal. But I wanted to set him on the right path, especially if I wasn't going to be there to guide him. Judy wholeheartedly agreed.

Although I denied it then, I was trying to put things in order and take care of my family while I still had time. The older kids knew I was sick. But Judy and I also wanted to keep things as normal as possible for them. So I took Brian to Canada.

The team recruiting Brian was the Acadie-Bathurst Titans in northern New Brunswick. Also drafted that year was Patrice Bergeron, who would go on to become a Stanley Cup winner with the Boston Bruins (his Titans' number, 37, was retired in 2011). Some other famous alumni of the Titans include Mario Lemieux, one-time player for (and now owner of) the Pittsburgh Penguins; and Olympic Gold Medalist and former Vancouver Canuck goalie Robert Luongo. In a piece of irony, Luongo was credited for getting the Canucks to game seven of the 2011 Stanley Cup Finals, only to lose to former teammate, Bergeron, and the Bruins.

Upon arrival at the airport, we were met by reporters, and by the team owner, Léo-Guy Morissette, a barrel-chested powerhouse known as one of the "kings" of the league— an outspoken man with a very colorful personality. He led us on a tour of the charming city on Chaleor Bay just south of Quebec Province, and then took us to the Titans' practice.

Brian actually got to skate while the owner and I watched. It was against NCAA rules for him to perform in full gear so he skated without it. I wanted to see for myself if he had what it takes to play at that level or if I was just being a wishful parent. It turned out that I wasn't. And it was a bittersweet moment. As I watched him fly around the ice, my heart was bursting with pride, but I wondered if I would see him skate next season.

The coaches really wanted Brian to stay and join the team, but he was uncertain. Neither Judy nor I was convinced that Brian was ready to live away from us, and we weren't comfortable having someone else raise our son. We didn't want him to waste his gift and felt that we could nurture it better than anyone else could. Besides, the college hockey system is just as good for launching a pro career. Going to Canada would mean forfeiting an education; there is life after hockey and Brian would need other skills someday. So I regretfully told Brian no.

While we were away, Kevin and Rita stayed home with Judy. Rita is Judy's younger sister and they are extremely close. They were born years apart, and Judy remembers Rita escaping her crib and crawling into bed with her when they were children. The bond between them goes back that far. Over the years, Kevin and I had spent a lot of time together—in the beginning, not always by choice. But he had become my very best friend and was completely devastated by my diagnosis.

In those anxious hours leading up to my surgery, Kevin felt there had to be *something* he could do, so he lay awake nights searching for a way to save my life. He kept asking himself, "What can I do to help Artie?" His answer came through the unofficial "Medjugorje Messengers," a group of local men who spread the word of hope in the most unlikely places.

Photo by Luca Lorenzi, courtesy of Wiki Commons.
The Village of Medjugorje.

5

Medjugorje Messengers

Rob Griffin first learned about the shrine in a locker room filled with twenty sweaty middle-aged men, including ten former NHL players, and three cases of beer. They had just finished a game. Rob was talking with his good friend, Jackie O'Donaghue, about Rob's father's recent cancer diagnosis. In front of this very macho audience, Jackie asked, "Griff, have you ever heard of a place called Medjugorje?"

Even before I got sick, God was setting in motion a plan to save me. It was like viral evangelization. My neighbor, Rob, first had to learn about Medjugorje to share it with Kevin, my brother-in-law, so he could share it with me. Like everything else in my story, it happened in a strange way.

Rob grew up in the little seaside community of Scituate. Often dubbed "the Irish Riviera," with its scenic harbor and commanding views of the Atlantic Ocean, it was once summer home to such Boston political heavyweights as Mayor James Michael Curley, as well as other "lace curtain" Irish wealthy enough to summer by the sea. In his youth, Rob ran with a rather wild crowd, and his stunts—including things like stealing a school bus—often captured the attention of local police. Yet through all the craziness, he was somehow drawn to his girlfriend Cathy's pious family. Rob remembers her grandmother saying the Rosary, and the prayerful atmosphere of their home, and thinking, "I want what they have." After graduating from Boston College, he married Cathy, and became a very successful businessman and a model citizen. Like me, Rob attended church with his family but never gave God much thought. Until his own father got sick. That sickness made him eager to hear the story of a man named Jackie O'Donaghue.

Jackie grew up in Scituate with Rob and they had known each other a long time. In the crowded locker room one day, after a hockey game, he told Rob about being healed of a shoulder injury in Medjugorje—where his parents had dragged him. Jackie had been the senior captain of a college hockey team that consistently made the NCAA championship. While celebrating his college's "Oktoberfest," he and his teammates decided to visit an all-girls school an hour away. Mere minutes into the trip there was an accident. Just before the crash, Jackie extended his arm to brace himself for impact. The force of the collision propelled two of his teammates from the back seat right through that arm, shattering the bones but leaving the ball in the socket of his shoulder. He endured six surgeries including bone grafts, and needed a full upper body cast with a bar from hip to elbow to keep his arm elevated. His hockey days were clearly over and he lost so much school time that he barely graduated with his class. Rob said that even after all the surgeries and intensive physical therapy, Jackie still had a "dead arm" that he could not raise above his head, an arm Rob found difficult to look at. For nine years, Jackie endured constant pain and relied on heavy doses of aspirin to get him through the day.

In the locker room he told Rob about the apparitions of the Blessed Virgin Mary and the miracles happening in a small Croatian village. When Jackie's parents had proposed a family trip to Medjugorje in 1991, Jackie was reluctant to go. It wasn't exactly a vacation and he didn't know what he would do there. But part of him was curious and he wondered if he might possibly experience a miracle of his own. Following a healing service where a renowned priest, Father Jozo, prayed over him, Jackie stood in the doorway of the church. It was there, he said, "I felt a warm pulsating wave through my left shoulder and down my arm, then another warm wave and then flows of heat from my left shoulder and arm. As I stood in that doorway, I lifted my arm up over my head for the first time since 1982. I could feel the snap-crackle-popping of the muscles stretching where they had atrophied before. I was in shock. The pulsating waves continued for hours." Not feeling worthy of this kind of healing, he was in denial and would not admit it right away. But a few days later, his wife Lisa told Sister Margaret Sims, the tour's spiritual advisor, of the healing. As Jackie recounts it, "My father had tears in his eyes, but Sister Margaret smiled like it was just another day in Medjugorje."

At this point the other players in the locker room were looking at Rob and Jackie as if they were crazy. Some even made snide comments. But Rob was unfazed. "If this place might heal my Dad, I was going to learn everything I could about it," he said.

Rob was never able to get his father overseas. But Jackie introduced him to Sister Margaret, who arranged for Maria Esperanza, a visionary and healer from Betania, Venezuela, to pray with him instead. (Maria would die in 2004, and in 2009 she would take the first step towards canonization, when she was declared a "Servant of God".) Seeing Maria was the closest Rob's father could come to a pilgrimage. Rob and his dad went to Betania II, a local retreat center, where Maria was visiting.

Rob's father wasn't physically healed, but other changes in him could be called miraculous. He had been an alcoholic for sixty years and Rob had not wanted him in his life. But after this prayer session his father quit drinking, came back to the family, and started attending daily Mass.

Rob was particularly impressed by the resilience of Sister Margaret's faith. Maria Esperanza had also prayed with Sister's own brother but he was not physically healed and died not long afterwards. As Rob says, "Many people would have given up on God because their prayers were not answered. Sister Margaret did not. Her devotion to the Lord never wavered."

While Rob did not experience a total conversion at this time, he did start attending Mass more often, even going Friday mornings when possible, and he made an effort to pray regularly. But he says, "If there was a hockey game on Sunday and I had to choose between that and Mass, hockey would usually win."

I did not know it then, but through these events, God was arranging my own healing and spiritual transformation. Jackie told Rob about Medjugorje and it wouldn't be long before Rob told Kevin. This couldn't have happened without that highly unlikely locker room conversation. God does indeed work mysterious ways.

I think I first learned about divine Providence in high school. As a camp counselor, I was working the pool one day, sitting in a chair observing the chaos, when something inside told me to get up and go to the edge of the water. When I looked down, I saw a four year old child lying in the bottom of the pool. I jumped in and pulled him out as adults rushed over to administer CPR. The little boy was saved. I don't know what told me to go over there, but I truly believe that it was the Holy Spirit, and I also believe that he is the one who sent us to Medjugorje. The seemingly chance meetings and conversations that got me there are just too unlikely to explain through mere serendipity.

The weekend before Labor Day, that same still, small voice was prompting my good friend Kevin. A few days earlier, he had been invited to play golf on Cape Cod by someone who had never asked him before. Kevin was randomly partnered with my Olmsted Drive neighbor, Rob Griffin, in the foursome. At this point he and Rob were just acquaintances. They met in a nearby town, where they left their cars to join their host for the one-hour ride to the course. In the car, Rob asked Kevin how I was doing. Kevin told him that the cancer was back and that my prognosis was poor. Rob was shocked. It was then that he told Kevin about Medjugorje. One of the players in the car groaned and asked them to change the subject. He had strong opinions about religion, none of them positive—and he let them know.

Kevin and Rob barely noticed his reaction. Totally engrossed in the subject of the Blessed Mother and miracles, they carried on through all eighteen holes, within earshot of other players. There were many raised eyebrows, and even some hostile comments from eavesdroppers, but Kevin and Rob didn't mind.

Kevin kept asking himself what he could do to save my life—not in an egotistical way. He was just desperate for a solution. After his talk with Rob he wondered about Medjugorje.

Kevin couldn't even spell the place, but with his wife's help at the computer, he found that thousands of other people apparently could, and there was a wealth of information on the topic. He wasn't one to surf the Internet, but he stayed on there spellbound for three hours that night. Kevin now believed that Medjugorje was the answer to his prayers and that he needed to get me there as soon as possible.

That pre-Labor Day weekend, Kevin did something risky and expensive: He reserved three first-class plane tickets to Medjugorje (he invited Rob to join us). That was an unusual invitation for a number of reasons. For one thing, Kevin did not know Rob very well. At the time, neither did I. In addition, both men ran very large companies. The trip would entail leaving the very next week, and "back to school" was a very hectic time in all of our families. But after discussing it with his wife, Rob called Kevin back and said yes.

Sister Margaret arranged pilgrimages to the shrine, so Rob asked for her help. She found us accommodations and made arrangements with local people to help us get around. She had us meet her at the Espousal Center in Waltham that week for Father Tom's children's healing service. That night he had the kids come up and put their hands on me to pray. It was incredibly moving to see the sincerity and faith in those innocent little faces.

However lovely that experience was, Sister Margaret had asked us to come for another reason: Apparently, she was concerned I might not be well enough to travel. Upon seeing me, she knew I was very sick, but judged that I could survive the trip. Sister Margaret had once again contacted her friend, Maria Esperanza, but this time on my behalf. Maria said she would hold me in prayer for the next three days and that I should definitely make the pilgrimage.

With my surgery less than two weeks away, our plans were set in motion. We were leaving the following Monday. As things turned out, Kevin's intervention didn't just change my life. It saved it.

Sunset from the window of Artie's British Airways flight to Medjugorje, via London.

6

September 4, 2000

I'm dying. And there's nothing anyone can do.

It was a tearful goodbye outside my home at 7 Olmsted Drive in Hingham, Massachusetts. In a neighborhood of leafy trees, manicured lawns, and beautiful homes with young children, we had built this house for our growing family six years ago. We'd envisioned a place where the kids could play pick-up basketball and street hockey in the driveway, and games of Wiffle ball and tag on the large front lawn. In good weather, Judy and I were always on the porch watching, and enjoying each other's company. This place held many happy memories.

On this perfectly clear, crisp New England fall day, my travel companions Kevin Gill and Rob Griffin arrived in a chauffeured black sedan. There were at least forty well-wishers, including neighbors, friends, and relatives. Many had tears in their eyes, looking at me as if I might never return. My entire family was present. And Rob's and Kevin's families also came for this last stop on the way to Boston's Logan International Airport. There was much hugging and kissing; the show of love and concern was overwhelming.

Our driver, Lloyd, had been told this departure might take a while, and he waited patiently while Judy blessed us with holy water, and then blessed Lloyd, too. Kevin distributed religious relics and rosary beads. And Rob presented a "healing cloth" from a Protestant minister who had suggested we meditate on the Acts of the Apostles, Chapter 11, as we pressed it against my chest. We were not sure about meditating because we had never done it, but we read the passage aloud in the car.

This was no ordinary trip. The next day we would arrive in Medjugorje, Bosnia-Herzegovina, in the former Yugoslavia, where we hoped to experience a miracle. I was very, very sick. In fact, I was dying. And I had been told there was nothing anyone could do. I had spent the last few weeks before the trip getting my affairs in order while trying anything that might save my life. I tried acupuncture, vitamins, herbs, and minerals. I sampled special teas, natural juices, and homeopathic medicine. And, much like last time, I had been prayed over, prayed for, and prayed with. But with only ten days until surgery, my condition had not changed. If anything, the fatigue had increased and I could barely get through the day. We did not know what to expect from this journey, but we knew it couldn't be any worse than sitting here waiting for the cancer to kill me.

The day I left was especially chaotic with packing and preparations. It was also the last day of summer vacation and with nine school-aged children, pandemonium ruled. I woke up that morning in full-out "get it done" mode, and spent the day readying myself for the journey ahead. Not knowing what to expect in a post-Communist country which had recently been an active war zone, I packed a week's worth of food and water.

I wished I could pull the family together and explain what I was doing, but I wasn't really sure myself. And this trip had come together so quickly that there wasn't much time. With children ranging in age from toddler to young adult, it would have been difficult to offer an age-appropriate group explanation and we didn't want to upset them. We would have time when I came home.

Judy and I had already learned the pitfalls of full medical disclosure. We always tried to be open and honest with the kids, so with my first cancer diagnosis we shared a detailed explanation of my upcoming kidney surgery. Five-year-old Gabrielle developed such severe stomach pains that we feared appendicitis—until Judy's friend, a nurse, suggested it might be from stress. She was right. Each of the children deals with things differently, and not knowing how it might affect them individually, we weren't going to overwhelm them again.

In the driveway, Rob and Kevin's kids were visibly upset; they did not want their fathers to go on this long trip to a foreign country. When Rob's four-year-old daughter, Casey, arrived at our house with her mother, she came running down the driveway and leapt into her father's arms. A precocious child, she had earlier hidden Rob's passport in an effort to keep him at home.

We had seldom traveled without our families so this was difficult. But more than that, the Gill and the Griffin children (unlike my own) were completely aware of my medical situation. They understood that this was a critical mission and they were very worried about the outcome.

In the year 2000, "Medjugorje" wasn't exactly a household word. Many people had heard of Lourdes and Fatima as places where the Blessed Mother had appeared to children in the nineteenth and twentieth centuries. But the Catholic Church hadn't officially approved Medjugorje as an apparition site—and still hasn't, although the Vatican is currently engaged in a thorough investigation.

Growing up, Judy's devout family often spoke of Lourdes and Fatima. My family, which was also Catholic, did not. Somewhere one of the nuns who taught me in school was turning in her grave, because while I knew of parish buildings by those names, I assumed they were named after donors or something. I knew nothing about Medjugorje either. I might as well have been flying to Bangladesh or Sri Lanka, but I was desperate enough to go anywhere to be healed.

Judy, generally a tower of strength, admitted that she was broken. I didn't know this side of Judy and seeing her fall apart was frightening. She was trying to hold it together for the kids, but she was clingy and emotional; part of me could not wait to be off with the guys where I could escape all the tears and the drama. Within 24 hours I would think back on this sentiment and chuckle.

She and I embraced one last time, and I said "I love you." She said she would be storming the heavens with prayer, and we agreed that this trip was part of God's plan. It all would be okay. I knew I had to go.

As the sedan pulled out of the long driveway, the images of the crowd receded behind the evergreens, and the last thing I saw was the small landscaped island in front of the house. I could no longer catch sight of my family. This was good because even with my resolve, if I had looked back at them, I might not have been able to leave.

When we reached the airport, tears of sadness turned to tears of laughter. After dinner in the British Airways Club, we boarded the Boeing 777 wide-bodied jet bound for London. It was 6 p.m. and we immediately donned the complimentary pajamas, startling the crew by wearing them during take-off. It's difficult to explain how ridiculous the three of us looked running around in identical sleepwear.

The seats resembled individual race cars equipped with personal video screens, toiletries kits, eye masks, as well as aromatherapy sprays for "stress relief" and "sleep." The amenities provided much laughter and we took turns spritzing one another and sampling the other goodies. After another meal, this time lobster and champagne, the seats folded into beds for the five-and-a-half-hour transatlantic flight. It was lights out for Rob and Kevin, but I couldn't sleep. Fortunately I had enough reading material to occupy me for the duration of the flight.

I took advantage of the time to read *Medjugorje, the Message*, by Wayne Weible. Published in 1985, it provides a history of the events at the shrine, and chronicles Weible's own experience of being "called" by the Blessed Mother. He reflects that it is never too late to convert and get closer to God. I couldn't put the book down. From the book I learned that on June 24, 1981, six farm children saw the shimmering figure of a woman high on a hill. With dark hair and blue eyes, she was wearing a silver grey gown and white veil, and carrying an infant in her arms. The next evening, the "Lady" returned and has appeared daily to one or more of the children (in their thirties at the time of this trip) ever since. I looked forward to learning more in the days to come.

I was already thinking about the changes I would make in my own life when I returned home. As we prepared to land, Rob showed us pictures of Medjugorje taken by his neighbor. In her photos, the image of the Virgin Mary can be clearly seen in the background. Rob's friend, like many others, had not actually seen her there but discovered her image when their film was developed back home. I wondered if we would find her in any of the pictures we would take this week.

In London's Heathrow Airport, we visited the British Airways Club to relax before the next leg of the journey. Because of issues with the computer monitor, we missed the boarding call and had to race down the long terminal corridors, nearly toppling other passengers to make our connection to Vienna. With only six days allotted for Medjugorje, and the scarcity of flights in and out, it was desperately important that we reach the gate before takeoff. It seemed Our Lady was protecting us already, because we made it just in time.

I had never been to Europe before. As we approached Vienna National Airport, seeing the pale pastel buildings, the serpentine Danube River, and the majestic mountains of Austria, I began to realize what I'd been missing. I'm not one of those Americans who mistake Disney Epcot for a Continental excursion, but I'm pretty basic and always thought we had everything we needed at home. Why did we need to go anywhere else? This now seemed ridiculous. I promised myself that if I lived, I would see as much of God's world as he permitted.

St. James Church, Main Street, Medjugorje.

7

Strangers in a Strange Land

Ireland has been described as having a "terrible beauty." In some ways, so does Bosnia.

61

Tyrolean Airlines took us from Vienna toward Mostar, a military airbase in Bosnia. The mountains there were rough, cutting, and barren, dotted with scrub trees resembling the small pines of Cape Cod. The plane was tossed by mountain winds as we descended and came to a grinding halt on the tarmac. Most commercial flights did not land here because it is quite dangerous. The planes come in over a cliff and must make a sudden drop to the runway as if the pilot were landing a helicopter instead of a jet.

The military presence was intimidating. At this time, Mostar still felt like a police state with armed militia everywhere. We'd had no idea of what to expect. I couldn't wait to take some pictures, but apparently this was forbidden. Just minutes into the country I nearly got strip-searched. When Kevin made the arrangements through his travel agent, he had asked for the closest airport to Medjugorje. Geographically this was it.

Sister Margaret had arranged for Martin Ilic, a former soccer star turned local innkeeper, to pick us up at the airport. He found us quickly, and helped put our bags into the trunk of his black Mercedes. It wasn't a new one, but we were surprised nonetheless. A young, dark-haired, athletic-looking man, Martin spoke surprisingly good English. His inn was full so he had arranged for us to stay at another guesthouse about a hundred yards away from his own. Virtually all of the accommodations in Medjugorje are family-owned and run, and we would be staying with Martin's good friends, Branco and Nevenka Cilic.

From the car, we saw bombed out homes, buildings torn apart, and devastated vegetation—all ravages of the recent war in Bosnia. However, our driver said that despite the devastating air attacks on the towns surrounding Medjugorje, it was never touched.

We asked about the yellow "crime tape" stretched across the sides of the roads and farmland. Martin explained that there were still vast areas of active minefields from the war that had ended five years earlier. The military did not have the equipment to detect and detonate the bombs, so all they could do was mark them.

Even though the conflict was over, we saw large tanks driving down the narrow streets and byways. We passed through three border checkpoints where soldiers wielding Uzis approached the car. Martin, who had been friendly and hospitable to this point, told us, "Hand over your passports, sit still, and shut up." We couldn't understand a word being said; it was like being in a scene from a World War II movie.

Thirty minutes after leaving Mostar, we arrived in the little village of Medjugorje. It was still daylight, and although we were exhausted, we could still appreciate the beauty of the mountains and the grape vineyards surrounding the town and its narrow main road. We caught a glimpse of the church farther down, as well as the silhouette of the large cross on the peak that dominated the valley.

There were military tanks here too, but they were from the United Nations and did not seem as menacing as the others. The car turned into a long narrow drive directly off the main street and Martin announced that we were now at the Cilic's guest house.

When we arrived at the inn, we were greeted warmly and shown to a small room with three beds, a window, and a bath. Rob predicted that rooming together would be a "very interesting experience," and he was right. Our accommodations were a cross between a hockey camp and a college dormitory, except that they were clean. Not plush, but livable. And it really didn't matter because we were there for one purpose only: to ask Our Lady's intercession for a miracle.

The Cilics, like many of the 5,000 residents of Medjugorje, had given up farming for the tourism industry. With the exception of a couple of small boutique-style hotels, accommodations in Medjugorje were quite basic. But things had improved significantly since the first visitors slept in St. James Church, or when, at Our Lady's request, villagers surrendered their own beds to pilgrims. Since then, residents had expanded their own homes, adding guestrooms for people from around the world. Bed and breakfasts like ours were equipped for group tours with twin beds or bunk lodging, utilitarian decor, and family style dining. There was little closet space, and guest phones and televisions were unheard of.

Each of us understood our mission—so fighting exhaustion, we dropped our bags and headed directly to St. James Cathedral just a few blocks away. We were told that the church fills up quickly, so we sprinted up the steps, across the plaza and entered through the large wooden doors. We'd learn later that James is the patron saint of pilgrims, millions of whom now came to this cathedral every year. I had read about the church on the plane. It was rebuilt in 1969 with nearly one thousand seats. But by the time of our trip in 2000, those seats were not enough. Regardless of season, time of day, or weather conditions, services at St. James were filled to capacity. I read that before the civil war, nearly two million faithful received Communion there each year and since the peace accord in 1995, the numbers had been rebounding to pre-war levels. In recent years the parish had added an outdoor altar with more than five thousand seats for summer visitors and festivals.

We were fifteen minutes early for the Rosary yet every single pew was full. People stood in the aisles, sat on the hard marble floor, and crowded every available space. There were many more people sitting on the outdoor benches where they could hear the Rosary and Mass on the PA system. I had never seen anything like this in my life; it was like Christmas and Easter combined. During the Rosary we were constantly interrupted by people squeezing in and out of the church doors, so we vowed to arrive even earlier the next time.

The people inside the church prayed—loudly! And after the first decade of the Rosary the church virtually exploded in song. It was the Ave Maria, and we looked at each other in astonishment over how enthusiastically and fervently they sang this hymn to Our Lady. It permeated the soul, practically lifting the worshiper out of his seat. American men don't really sing in church. *We* certainly didn't. But here? These people were so engaged you'd think they were on the sidelines at the Super Bowl. There were some thirty priests on the altar and I thought to myself that Mass at the Vatican could not be any more impressive.

The Rosary and Mass were in Croatian, but while we did not understand a word, the music was beautiful and lifted our spirits. We left church on an emotional high.

One of the major messages of Medjugorje is forgiveness. For Catholics, this means seeking pardon from a priest. None of us three had been to Confession in years, but we had come to Medjugorje in search of healing and the books we read said that penance is essential. There were twenty outdoor confessionals staffed by visiting priests who spoke a variety of languages. Hundreds of people were standing in line, some of whom said they had been waiting for an hour or more. That was something else we'd never seen happen in America.

As we waited, we estimated that between the three of us, we had a combined fifty years' worth of sins to confess, and jokingly wondered what time the confessionals closed.

All kidding aside, it was a little intimidating speaking face to face with an unfamiliar priest. But he was very reassuring and the experience was surprisingly comfortable. I don't remember ever feeling so "clean" as I did afterwards: more than fifteen years of sins erased.

At dinner back at the inn, we met Zeljka, the guide Martin had arranged for the next few days. She spoke enough English for us to converse. And she was extremely knowledgeable about the apparitions.

Zeljka is a first cousin of Vicka, the visionary whom Sister Margaret had asked to pray with me, and although Zeljka had never seen the Blessed Mother herself, she had grown up with all the visionaries. She was fourteen when the apparitions began and was there on the hill the second day after Our Lady first appeared in 1981. She told us how other children envied the visionaries—who were stunned at the responsibility that was suddenly placed on them. The Blessed Mother chose ordinary children for visionaries, just as she had at Lourdes and Fatima. Yet everyone expected them to be saints, and they were not.

Interestingly enough, when the apparitions began these children knew even less about Lourdes and Fatima than I did. In fact, they had never heard of either event when they saw the Blessed Mother on the hill that day.

Zeljka had been with Vicka during her apparitions for many years. At her own Confirmation, she was allowed to see a sparkling aura when Our Lady was present, but it was the only time she had seen anything supernatural. She added that the Blessed Mother had been dictating her autobiography to Vicka, little by little, for many years and would tell Vicka when it was time to share it. Zeljka was present for a session one day and remembered being able to see Vicka's writing in a floral notebook. She was incredibly excited that she could read the contents, until the apparition ended and her mind was "wiped clean." Much to her disappointment, she could remember nothing.

But it was getting late and Zeljka promised to tell us more of the story in the days to come. I had barely slept in the twenty-seven hours since we left Hingham, and Kevin and Rob threatened to put me down with a tranquilizer gun. It wasn't necessary. Totally exhausted, I fell into a deep but fitful sleep.

Vicka praying over Artie in Leo's Jewelry Store, Medjugorje, September 2000
Rob Griffin and Kevin Gill in background (L and R)

8

Visit with a Visionary

In my dream, my father is holding me in the freezing cold water of Carson Beach in South Boston. I'm terrified. I try to kick and flail my arms but I am over my head and hanging on for dear life in the choppy water, resisting with all my might. Finally he gives up. I cry because all I want to do is please him.

It wasn't the best night's sleep. Rob complained that the blankets were so small it was like sleeping under a washcloth, while Kevin's snoring sounded like a wounded sea lion.

A blinding headache kept me in bed until just before morning Mass. We arrived early enough to get seats because the German Mass had not yet ended. In addition to German, they had daily Masses in English, Italian, and Croatian. Again, there were many visiting priests concelebrating, and the congregation's participation was inspiring.

Outside, Zeljka had some bad news. Vicka had been called away to Rome the previous night. She had a friend who was ill and she had gone to pray with her. This was a huge setback. We had been told Medjugorje was a healing place in and of itself, but we felt that Vicka's prayers would have been a direct connection to the Virgin Mary. Vicka has been tasked by the Blessed Mother to pray especially for the sick and we'd been counting on her presence. We were all disappointed. However, we had come a long way to be with Mary and couldn't let this deter us.

We regrouped at Café Dubrovnik, an open air restaurant across the street. It was our first morning there, but we already missed our families, so we asked Zeljka where we could buy them some gifts.

Leo's was a small shop on Main Street, alongside many others that had opened since the massive tourist influx of the last eighteen years. Its glass cases were filled with every kind of religious jewelry and artifacts: medals, bracelets, crosses, and rosary beads. With the number of people for whom I needed to buy things, I realized that this morning was going to be expensive. Then I remembered the kind of money I routinely spent on hockey skates, sticks and other sporting goods. That put things in perspective.

My normal shopping consists of walking into a store and walking out within minutes. Hunt, capture, leave. Yet we had been scanning the racks for 45 minutes when we heard Zeljka exclaim, "Vicka is here!" She had missed her flight and had come to buy a gift for her friend en route to the airport. We rushed up to her, and this tiny, frail, dark haired woman agreed to pray over me right there in the store. Observers poured in from the street as she asked Kevin and Rob to put their hands on me. I've never seen anyone pray with such intensity. It was air-conditioned, yet my body became so hot that my friends broke out in a sweat. Kevin later told me that Vicka was gripping my head so hard that her arm muscles were actually bulging. We all became very emotional. Before leaving, she promised to say a special prayer for me in Rome later that evening, during the time when Our Lady appeared to her.

Next Zeljka brought us to Apparition Hill, formerly called Crnica, where the visionaries first saw Mary floating above a cloud before ascending to the summit. We passed under the brightly colored awnings of the open air shops lining the side of the steep paved walkway. Many merchants sat outside their stores with their display racks of glittering beads, jewelry and local crafts. The reddish pavement sidewalk bordering the commercial buildings was cracked from the heavy foot traffic.

After about fifty yards the paved surface ended and we started up the mountain, snaking between rocks and thorn bushes, frequently grasping stumps and branches to keep from slipping. It looked a lot easier than it was, and we talked about how grueling this walk must be in the rain. Fortunately the sun was with us and we were on an incredible high from Vicka's prayers. I felt jet-propelled, as if I could do *anything*.

On the way up, Zeljka told us about the early days of the apparitions, which began on June 24, 1981:

It was around 6 p.m. on the Feast of John the Baptist when fifteen-year-old Ivanka Ivankovic[1] and sixteen-year-old Mirjana Dragicevic were on their way home from a walk near the hill known as Podbrdo. Ivanka happened to look up and saw a luminous figure she immediately recognized as "Gospa" (the Croatian term for the Blessed Mother), and called out to Mirjana to look. Mirjana thought Ivanka was imagining things and kept on walking.

They then came upon the twelve-year-old shepherdess Milka Pavlovic, who asked them for help gathering her sheep. As they turned back towards the

---

1   Although many of the children have the same last name, with the exception of Milka and Marija none are related.

hill with her, Ivanka once again saw the woman holding a baby and now the others did too.

Then sixteen-year-old Vicka Ivankovic, who had come looking for her friends Ivanka and Mirjana, found them staring at the top of the hill. Mirjana told Vicka to look, but she was afraid. So she ran back towards the village.

Before she got there, she saw twenty-year-old Ivan Ivankovic and sixteen-year-old Ivan Dragicevic carrying apples from the orchards. Vicka told them about the vision and asked them to go back with her.

When they got to the hill, Vicka could see the Lady, too. The younger Ivan was so frightened that he jumped over a fence and ran away, spilling all his apples. The older Ivan could only make out something white. Although the Lady was beckoning the children to come closer, they were too afraid to move. Instead, they retreated home—where no one believed them, and their families teased them mercilessly.

The children returned the next day hoping to see the Lady again. The story had already spread in the small village and some of the curious followed along. There was a sudden flash of light and she appeared to the visionaries once more, this time without the Infant. Those who saw her said that she was smiling and was beautiful beyond words. She extended her hand beckoning them closer. So they rushed up the hill towards her, falling to their knees and praying the Our Father, Hail Mary and Glory Be. Given the *heavy incline and sharp rocks, it's hard to imagine how the visionaries reached the top as quickly as reported through the dense brush and boulders that were there at the time. One observer said that it should have taken more than ten minutes to reach the top, but that they climbed it in two. Some claim that they ran up the hill, while the visionary Ivan says that they were "carried" up the hill by a supernatural force.*

That day the Lady spoke for the first time—praying with them except during the Hail Mary. Milka and the older Ivan had not come and would never see her again. Milka's older sister, Marija, and ten-year-old Jacov Colo came instead. They became the fifth and sixth visionaries.

As the Lady disappeared, she said, "God be with you, my angels."

That morning of our first day in Medjugorje, Kevin, Rob and I climbed this same hill, navigating the large rocks made smooth by all the pilgrims who have crossed them. The walk was tedious, and we understood the crowd's astonishment at how easily and quickly the visionaries had made their ascent.

About halfway to the top, Zeljka pointed to a spot off to the right marked with a simple cross. After leaving the summit on the third day of the apparitions, visionary Marija felt pushed to the side of the trail by an invisible force. Our Lady was standing in front of a wooden cross and crying and pleading *"Mir, mir, mir!"* ("Peace, peace, peace!") The rest of her message was this: "Be reconciled! Only Peace. Make your peace with God and among yourselves. For that, it is necessary to believe, to pray, to fast, and to go to Confession." It seems that Our Lady's message went unheeded, because ten years later on that very day the Bosnian war began.

Sixteen million pilgrims had already climbed Apparition Hill before our own visit. During the day this trip could be painfully slow because of the large tour groups. The pilgrims would form a human barrier across the path as they listened to their guides and stopped to pray beneath the bronze relief plaques or to photograph the panoramic valley below. The slope had a perfect view of red clay-roofed homes and wineries set in a landscape of green fields and tidy rows of grapes. But Apparition Hill was not overly crowded that day and we were able to keep moving. While pilgrims flock to Medjugorje year-round, the largest crowds arrive during the summer. It may not have been peak season, but the village was still very busy when we were there.

We finally approached the crest of the hill where the Madonna had appeared. Today there is a magnificent white stone statue there, but it wasn't there yet when we visited. At the top, Zeljka led us in the "Peace Rosary" taught to the visionaries by Our Lady. It consists of one Our Father, one Hail Mary, and one Glory Be, repeated seven times. The sun was warm and the view was magnificent. No one wanted to leave. There was an overwhelming sense of peace, and I already felt that I was in Our Lady's presence.

On the way down, we noticed people picking up stones. Zeljka advised us to gather five small rocks from the side of the hill. She explained that the Blessed Mother has given us five "weapons" against Satan. Each pebble represents one of those weapons, and Our Lady's call for us to embrace them is the main message of Medjugorje. Those weapons are:

- Prayer, especially with one's family.
- Bible reading daily.
- Confession, at least once a month.
- Fasting, especially on the Church's traditional days of Wednesday and Friday.
- The Eucharist, received daily if possible.

Zeljka said we should display these rocks in our homes as reminders of Our Lady's requests. As we continued down the path, we collected some more for our families and friends, promising to share the stones' significance as well.

My spirits were lifted, and after visiting the shops at the base, we stopped for lunch at a restaurant on the side of the road. It was rustic in appearance, all exposed wood and beams, and like many of the eateries here, it was open air. Between the hanging plants and foliage, we watched crowds of people arriving and departing the mountain—including the very determined sick and handicapped people working their way to the top, some of them barefoot or on their knees.

Before the trip the three of us had never shared anything spiritual. Kevin and I were close, but I don't ever remember talking about faith in more than a superficial way. We knew that Rob was Catholic, and that was all. He was still just an acquaintance, but a very compatible traveler.

During our lunch conversation, the three of us realized that we had a lot in common. Each of us was happily married and had met his wife in high school. Our families were the most important things in our lives and we spent as much time with them as possible. We all came from humble beginnings and each of us ran a large company.

After working at FEDEX, I had started a successful trucking business. When I was first married, I did whatever job was necessary to pay the bills but with Judy's help, I was finally able to start my own business.

Kevin owned McCusker-Gill, the largest sheet metal construction company in New England. He started in the office of an engineering company, quickly moved to apprentice, then graduated to drafting and estimating. After a few years he took a chance and bought out another company. Many people depended on him for their livelihood so it was very difficult for him to get away. For that reason this trip was especially meaningful.

Rob was the president of Cushman and Wakefield, Boston's largest commercial real estate brokerage. From our conversations it seemed he was equally driven in both work and play. Unlike Kevin and me, Rob was a self-professed fitness fanatic who consistently ate healthy. There was a limited food selection in Medjugorje, and he has some serious food allergies, so the trip was especially difficult for him. I was moved by his generosity in coming on this pilgrimage.

Of the three of us, it turned out Rob was the most spiritually advanced, yet we were all discovering new things on this pilgrimage. We discussed our experiences so far, and Kevin admitted that he had struggled with doubts about God's existence shortly before the trip. His experiences so far had helped to quell his uncertainty, and he couldn't wait to tell his wife Rita about his revitalized faith. Our eyes had already been opened in many ways. But the story was just beginning.

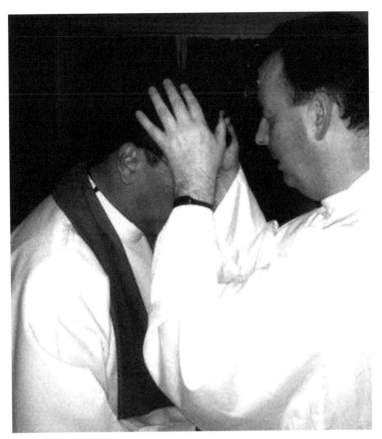

Father Simon Cadwallader praying with a pilgrim.

9

Forgiveness

"Take Jesus into you each time you receive and ask him to heal you. The Eucharist will destroy the cancer."

It was just a little over a week until my surgery. I tried not to think about it, but the setting sun reminded me that the days were quickly passing. That night we attended the Rosary followed by Mass, then Adoration at 10 p.m. Although we arrived 30 minutes early this time, the only seat we could find was on the hard marble floor between the first pew and the altar. We sat or kneeled on that floor for the next 90 minutes. The songs were in different languages with the lyrics projected on a large screen beside the altar. We didn't know what we were singing, but it didn't matter. Kevin whispered he was reminded of his teacher, Sister Marie, who quoted St. Augustine to the effect that when you sing, you pray twice. I certainly hoped so.

As moved as I was by the music and the electric atmosphere in the church, I wasn't feeling well and it was getting extremely uncomfortable on the floor. I thought about leaving. But my eyes were drawn to the Host which was more than eight inches wide and encircled in an enormous gold monstrance that glistened like rays of the sun. When I clearly saw the silhouette of the face of Christ on the Host, I was transfixed, and decided to stay for the duration.

The seers say that Our Lady has been communicating "secrets," predictions of events the world cannot know in advance. Ivanka, Jacov and Mirjana have each received ten secrets and no longer have daily apparitions. Ivanka and Jacov see Our Lady only once a year. Mirjana sees Our Lady on the second day of each month. She has her apparition at the Blue Cross where pilgrims gather to witness. Ivan, Marija, and Vicka have gotten nine secrets, and do not know when, or if, they will receive ten. The Blessed Mother has told the visionaries that when the Medjugorje apparitions cease, she will leave a permanent mark to prove her presence here.

Ivanka spoke to a group of twenty-five people through an interpreter. Ivanka recounted that when the apparitions began, she was living with her grandmother because her mother had passed away. The fearless Ivanka asked Our Lady for a message from her departed mother. The Madonna passed along this simple request, "Obey your grandmother because she is old." Since then, Our Lady has taken Ivanka to visit her mother in heaven five times. She says that Our Lady has shown her pictures of heaven and hell and that two of the visionaries have seen heaven, hell and purgatory.

After lunch Zeljka brought us to a talk by Father Slavko Barbaric. We entered a bright and airy space referred to as the "Yellow Conference Hall" behind St. James Cathedral. Its front wall was dominated by an original painting, "Our Lady of Medjugorje," that the visionaries say most accurately depicts the Blessed Virgin Mary. She is beautiful with long dark hair, blue eyes, and an expression of perfect love on her face. She hovers on a cloud above St. James Cathedral surrounded by an azure sky, her arms outstretched as if to welcome pilgrims. The twelve-by-six-foot masterpiece was painted in 1998 by the famous Florentine artist Carmelo Puzzolo, also the sculptor of the many exquisite bronze plaques that line the trails of Apparition Hill and Cross Mountain. Puzzolo's depiction of Our Lady is the most recognizable icon of the apparition.

Father Slavko was a Franciscan priest who came to Medjugorje two years after the apparitions began. He wrote many books that have been translated into more than twenty languages. His most popular book is called *Pray with the Heart*, whose message he laid out in the talk that day. The three of us would not comprehend its meaning until later, during our fateful journey up Cross Mountain. An inspiration to millions of pilgrims, Father showed such powerful reverence for the Eucharist that he resembled a saint having raptures, like the pictures on prayer cards. We wondered if this man would be a saint himself someday.

Father spoke reverently about Mary and her teachings. He emphasized the positive approach; the importance of praise instead of ridicule. He said that if you are teaching a child to walk and he falls, you have two choices. You can clap and praise him, or ask him why he fell. He assured us that Our Lady believes in praise: "If we say one Hail Mary, she doesn't ask why we didn't say more. She is pleased with our effort and supports us to do better. She loves us unconditionally and wants us to know she is our mother."

Sadly, two months following our visit Father Slavko died of a heart attack after leading his weekly stations of the cross on Mt. Krizevac. The next day, Our Lady told Ivan, "I rejoice with you and desire to tell you that your brother Slavko has been born into heaven and intercedes for you."

After the talk we approached the rectory where Father Jozo Zovko lived, and where the visionaries experienced many apparitions. Zeljka stopped outside and gave us the next installment of the events of June 1981.

On June 26, Mary appeared on the hill for the third evening in a row. As the apparitions continued, pressure on the children and Father Jozo was building. In Communist Yugoslavia, no religious assembly was allowed outside of a church building, and anyone who defied this edict would be subject to arrest and very heavy fines. As pastor, Father Jozo was worried about the ramifications for everyone if this situation continued, so he vigorously interrogated all the seers. They were unshakeable. Their stories were consistent; all described the Blessed Mother's appearance exactly the same way, and said that she spoke in a "singing voice."

Things only got worse for Father Jozo. Despite the sweltering heat the crowd on the hill reached 5,000 the fourth night. Following the flashes of light, the Blessed Mother appeared, then vanished because the crowd was trampling on her long veil, then reappeared. Finally some villagers formed a circle around the children to give them some space. The visionaries begged the Madonna for a sign to prove their truthfulness but she replied, "My angels, do not be afraid of injustices. They have always existed." As she left them she said, "Farewell, my angels. Go in the peace of God."

Word spread further. People were flooding into the small village and the next day 15,000 assembled to witness the apparition. Father Jozo still did not believe the children and was increasingly angry. Meanwhile the Communist government was bearing down, warning him of "dire consequences" if he did not control the situation. To make matters worse, the visionaries had begged Our Lady to heal a little boy. As his condition showed miraculous improvement, media outlets from all over Yugoslavia, and then from Italy, started flocking to Medjugorje.

The children were taken to police stations in several cities, and then driven to the hospital for medical and psychiatric exams. Although subjected to every type of intimidation, they did not back down. The doctors concluded that they were normal, well-adjusted children and sent them home.

By evening, the police had surrounded Ivan's house, frightening his mother into keeping him home. But Our Lady appeared to Ivan by himself later that evening. She told him, "Be at peace and take courage," and then smiled at him before she left. He was allowed to accompany the others after that.

The military police were everywhere, threatening, barring doors and promising severe repercussions. They dispatched an ardent atheist doctor to an apparition, where she asked to touch Our Lady. With the Madonna's permission, Vicka placed the doctor's hand on her veil and the doctor looked as if she'd been struck by lightning. She rushed to the foot of the hill to tell the waiting government officials that she would not participate in the investigation.

Through it all, Our Lady protected the children. The communists sent social workers to detain them so they would miss their evening apparition. They did not miss it, and whatever the social workers experienced caused them to resign the next day. At one point, the police kidnapped several of the seers but Our Lady appeared to them in the van. The expressions on their faces scared their captors into releasing them.

A consistent message from the early apparitions was that Medjugorje's priests were to "perservere in the faith and protect the faith of the people." And while Father Jozo was not a believer, Our Lady would ensure that he protected them as well. Despite the persecution he would endure, in time he would become their fiercest ally.

When we returned to the Cilics' from our afternoon at St. James, Kevin surprisingly said he "forgot a few things" in Confession and must return. Not wanting to miss dinner, Rob and I stayed behind as Kevin headed back to church.

A while later, he burst into the room as charged up as I have ever seen him and said, "Come on boys, you're coming with me!" He had met a wonderful priest named Father Simon Cadwallader, from Liverpool, England and said that he had just had an "amazing confession." Those were strange words coming from Kevin. He said that Father's goal was to "make sure that at the end, I felt completely clean and free of sin." He said Father Cadwallader would only be there for five more minutes so we'd better hurry.

So we rushed back to "Confessional Row." The irony was that we hadn't been to Confession in more than fifteen years and now the three of us were sprinting down the main street of Medjugorje to confess yet again. Most of the lines were very long, but oddly enough, there was no wait for the English booth... so in I went.

Father Simon was clearly a special priest. His gentle blue eyes and open face were full of compassion and I immediately felt comfortable. He was soft-spoken with an easy, spiritual manner that allowed you to open up and confess with your heart, which is what the sacrament is all about. I told him about my cancer and he prayed over me. He emphasized the words of the Our Father, "thy will be done," and told me to prepare for anything. He reminded me of the next phrase: "on earth as it is in heaven," pointing out that there is no cancer in heaven.

Father Simon told me the Eucharist is the most powerful medicine on earth. He said, "Take Jesus into you each time you receive and ask him to heal you. The Eucharist will destroy the cancer." Lastly, Father Simon gave me absolution, saying, "Listen for God's word. I forgive you for everything you have done since you were an adolescent, as if you were God's newborn baby. If you feel you've hurt anyone, just once, ask God to heal the scars you've caused, and know that he will."

Forgiveness, forgiving yourself and others, is important to people of all faiths. But I was learning that Confession is not optional for Catholics. It is a sacrament just like Baptism, Confirmation, and Matrimony, and through it as through them we receive a grace given to us by Jesus. I used to see Confession as a simple recitation of sins and absolution from the priest—kind of a laundry list of things I'd done wrong. That day I realized it was so much more, a conversation with Jesus through the person of the priest. Why did I stay away for so many years?

After that confession, I felt completely relaxed. I began to realize that healing isn't about winning. It's about surrendering. I consciously surrendered it all to God, and knew I would have a more restful night's sleep.

When I stepped out of the confessional, Rob went in. Kevin and I stood back to give him some privacy. There was enough space between the door and the line that you couldn't really hear what was being said. But as Kevin and I waited outside, we heard someone roaring with laughter right through the walls. In fact, the laughter carried right across the courtyard. We were surrounded by Germans and Italians who all started staring at us, and we both wondered what on earth was going on. When Rob came out he told us, "It was the *priest* who was laughing."

He described a very similar experience with Father Simon, saying he was "the most fantastic priest I've ever met." It was as if Father had arranged his entire evening for us—spending close to an hour with each of us in confession. At the time we had no way of knowing the role that Father Simon would play in our lives. In fact, in the years to come, he would become part of our families.

Back in our room we discussed the day's events and wrote in our journals. This had become our regular bedtime practice and we discovered we could open up and share spiritually in ways we had never done with anyone else, even our wives. I heard the bells of St. James chime softly as I drifted off to sleep.

Blue Cross on Apparition Hill.
Back row: Zeljka and Rob
Front Row: Artie and Kevin.

10

The Triumph of the Cross

I'm not much on male affection, but the three of us were hugging, crying, and yelling at the top of our lungs. In the pouring rain at the top of Cross Mountain, we begged God for my healing.

We prepared for a rainy climb up Cross Mountain. In 1933 the villagers dragged cement up the steep rocky peak to build the huge 16,000-ton cross that is visible from every point in the village. It contains a relic of the True Cross donated by Pope Pius XI.

Prior to its construction, many unusual hailstorms had destroyed the crops of the impoverished farmers. Once the cross stood, the storms ceased and the harvest was never harmed again. It became traditional to celebrate Mass atop Cross Mountain in September on the Feast of the Triumph of the Cross. The communists outlawed religious gatherings outside of churches, but for this one day each year they made an exception.

The night before the first apparition a great storm enveloped the village of Medjugorje, with thunder and lightning illuminating the cross. While the rain that set in the afternoon that we climbed was not of this magnitude, it made for a difficult trek. From below, the trail resembles peanut brittle, and looks just about as easy to navigate, but we soon discovered why Zeljka discouraged tonight's excursion. So many people have climbed the path that the craggy rocks have been polished smooth, and when they are wet, they are as slippery as ice. The pitch was so sharp that some guides recommended gloves to get a better vertical grip, but with only two days remaining, we were so anxious to experience Cross Mountain that we had made no special provisions. As on Apparition Hill, we had heard some make the trip in their bare feet as an additional penitential offering. I was unable to imagine that. The walk was hard enough in shoes.

The edges of the trails were laced with pine trees and in the dampness, their scent filled the air. When we had passed the entrance earlier, we'd read the brown, hand-painted sign suggesting that pilgrims would be "accompanying Jesus as he carries his cross." During the climb, I was reminded of my grueling physical and emotional journey of the last twelve months, and the symbolism was not lost on me. As we passed the bronze reliefs of Jesus' sorrowful walk to Calvary, I noticed that so many pilgrims had touched his shoulder that the finish had worn away. It shone brightly, contrasting the smallness of his shoulder against the enormous cross. I wondered how many of these pilgrims had been battling handicaps or illnesses like mine, and I hoped that they had found consolation here.

I felt that we were being led up the mountain by Our Lady herself. She had reportedly appeared on this mountain numerous times and there had been unusual phenomena witnessed and photographed by many people. She had told the visionaries that the construction of the cross was providential and that pilgrims and villagers should go here often to pray.

Beneath us, so many worshippers filled St. James Cathedral that the services had to be broadcast on loudspeakers for the overflow crowds. The sound of the hymns floated up the side of the hill, which I found very comforting. Other than the music, the valley was completely still.

Generally, it takes about an hour to reach the top because pilgrims stop to pray at each of the Stations of the Cross. Our hearts were full of prayer, but we were fast approaching darkness and stopped just long enough to touch each station along the way. There would be no moon that night and although the trail had been worn down by the sixteen million people who came before us, we knew it would be very easy to get lost or injured.

About halfway up the mountain I felt a searing pain in my right lung, a pain I could literally put my finger on, and Kevin and Rob had to wait for me to catch my breath. I thought to myself, "Oh dear God, it's getting worse!" I feared that I might not make it to the top and remembered that the only way down was on foot. Kevin and Rob were trading worried looks but there was nothing they could do to stop me. I persevered, wondering if the specific location of the pain meant something was happening to the tumor. Desperate for a miracle, I hoped so.

When we reached the top, we began to pray. The rain had let up temporarily. It was misting and grey and wonderfully peaceful, and we were the only ones left at the foot of the cross. This was remarkable because it's not unusual for there to be as many as 30,000 people on the mountain at any given time. The posted signs demand total silence, but Zeljka had warned us that people didn't always comply, so we were very fortunate to have this quiet time for reflection. We tried to beseech God with all our hearts, as Father Slavko had instructed us. It was the first time in our lives we'd had the courage to pray like this. We rarely allowed ourselves public emotional displays. Even in private, we avoided them. They just weren't manly. But this time, for once, I acknowledged my weakness and humbled myself. In fact, I lay down prostrate in the mud at the foot of the cross. There was no cure for my disease. My survival depended on God, and God alone. I thought I had learned this at Mission Church when I felt I'd been "hit" during the healing service, but on top of that mountain I finally understood. I wept in desperation and begged for God's mercy.

The three of us were on our hands and knees on the hard rocks, hugging and crying as the rain resumed and puddles formed on the ground around us. Since we were there alone and disturbed no one, we yelled at the tops of our lungs, holding onto one another, begging the Lord to bring me back to my family healed. Rob remembered the prayer, "Ask and you shall receive, seek and you shall find," and we stormed heaven, shouting those words until we were hoarse. We had come to claim my healing and we were certain God heard our prayers in this sacred place. Who knew how he would answer them? Yet at that moment, it didn't matter. A sense of peace overcame us. This moment will stay with each of us for the rest of our lives.

Earlier I had been concerned about the walk down the mountain, but the pain in my lung had subsided. Having experienced the wonders of this place, I trusted that Our Lady would take care of us. We were silent as we navigated the trail down hill, each lost in his thoughts. There was no one to disturb us.

That night we journeyed alone up to Apparition Hill. We prayed in the drizzling mist at the top before heading down the other side to the "Blue Cross." This was where the visionaries used to meet secretly for their apparitions during the communist persecution. The site was now marked with a simple wooden cross and a statue of Our Lady. (There is no particular significance to the cross's color. Blue was the only shade of paint available the day they built it.) Several wooden benches made of it a small outdoor chapel. The usual dozen or so tour buses were absent and we had the place to ourselves.

We paused for a moment in the evening stillness. Our Lady's sculpted stone hands held a broken rosary. That seemed wrong. Rob said, "Artie, Our Lady shouldn't have broken beads. You should give her yours." I hesitated because my rosary was a gift from Rita and Kevin, and I quietly explained this to Rob. Zeljka overheard, and handed me a white plastic set which I reverently placed in Our Lady's hands. We offered our petition again, praying with the heart, "Ask and you shall receive, seek and you shall find." Sometime after 9:00 p.m., Zeljka urged us to get out of the rain.

The next morning, September 8, Mary's birthday, was a very important feast day in Medjugorje. We arrived early at St. James before the end of the Croatian Mass. It was different. Women in kerchiefs with Slavic faces filled the church, many standing at the back, uttering the responses in soft but fervent voices. They dressed very simply, a reflection of the "old" Medjugorje in the midst of the current wave of tourism. Many had come in from their farms and vineyards.

After Mass we ran into Father Simon. We had a chance to say goodbye and asked for his contact information. He'd made such an impression on us that we hoped to stay in touch. We also spotted Father McDonough from Boston, the priest who had prayed over me at Mission Church last December. We'd had no idea that he would be here. I asked him to pray with me. We learned that he was on the same tour that Sister Margaret had booked for us that afternoon, so we headed over to the bus together. We were traveling to hear Father Jozo Zovko.

Throughout this trip some guiding force seemed to point us towards people who had experienced miracles in Medjugorje. One of them was Ray Baril, who was on his third trip. He told us his story as we waited to board the bus. He was once gravely ill with a rare form of celiac disease. His wife arranged a family Medjugorje pilgrimage that he didn't want to take. He deferred to her, but got cold feet and walked off the plane before take-off. Realizing he had inadvertently taken his daughter's luggage, he re-boarded and the cabin doors closed before he could exit. Once in Medjugorje, he was miserable. There were no flights home, so one afternoon he went to a local chapel to escape the intense summer heat. Something happened there that he would only describe as a conversion experience, and he sat there for hours, arriving back at the guest house just before dinner. His wife could sense that something changed in him. He had lost all interest in leaving. She was convinced that he was physically healed, so she tested this thesis by planting a small piece of barley in his meal—something that normally would have caused debilitating diarrhea. He didn't get sick. And he never would again.

As Ray finished his story, the driver opened the doors and we climbed aboard to sit with Father McDonough, and a Father McNamara—who was also from Boston. We soon departed for our visit with Father Jozo, some 35 minutes away.

Our tour guide introduced herself and recounted the dire consequences Father Jozo had experienced for his stance on the apparitions. He had initially concluded that the visionaries were lying. But one morning as he was praying, Our Lady appeared to him and said, "Protect the children." A moment later they came running into the church with communist soldiers in hot pursuit. Instantly, he realized that they were telling the truth, and so he did as Mary asked, and stood up for them. This cost him greatly. He was subject to interrogations and beatings at the hands of the government, as well as vehement opposition from his own bishop in Mostar. The bishop, afraid of retribution, wanted no trouble with communist leaders and ordered Father Jozo to stop the children from speaking about the apparitions. He would not. When he refused to renounce the apparitions and halt the crowds pouring into Medjugorje, the Yugoslav army boarded up St. James and sentenced him to three years of hard labor. Popular pressure forced his early release, and he became a hero to the people of Medjugorje. After his sentence was commuted, he was reassigned to his current parish, Blessed Assumption in Siroki Brijeg.

On our way to that church, everyone prayed together as we made our peaceful trip through the mountains of Bosnia and Croatia. The limestone brick church topped a hill overlooking the countryside, with twin towers that reminded me of the spires of St. James in Medjugorje. Our guide told us that it was Romanesque architecture; I took her word for it. From the front it actually looked a bit like Mission Church in Boston.

Several tourist buses were already there and as we waited for them to leave, I managed to separate from the group and find a spot overlooking the valley where I could reflect and pray. Although I was thoroughly enjoying the time with my friends, I relished this quiet period alone. I became very emotional, which was not unusual for me anymore.

When the last bus pulled out, we went inside the church, where Zeljka had saved front row seats for us. Blessed Assumption was a large church with high vaulted ceilings, and an altar illuminated by rose windows with a brightly painted statue of Mary about ten feet tall. Father Jozo spoke through an interpreter named Nancy Latta. He wore the traditional brown Franciscan robe and sandals. He spoke with a quiet intensity, pausing to emphasize his words, and punctuating them with gentle but deliberate hand motions. Nancy, whom Zeljka described as a native Croat who had practiced law in Canada, spoke beautifully and with great emotion.

Father Jozo's talk made us uncomfortable because it seemed directed at us. He was like a modern day John the Baptist, scolding us for how we lived our lives in the West. Some people walked out and we were tempted to join them, but we stayed out of respect. He spoke about the importance of prayer, about his troubles in the early years of the apparitions, and about what Our Lady asks of us. He distributed beautiful icons of Mary, and rosary beads blessed during an apparition. He asked us to place the image on our hearts and to pray, inviting her in.

The laying on of hands is one of the oldest traditions in Christianity, with roots in Jewish beliefs and practice. It is believed to be a sacred source of healing. I closed my eyes as I waited for Father's blessing. He gave me a couple of taps on the cheek and said in decent English, "Hey, I'm praying over you!" Yet another person was striking me to get my attention. I found myself smiling as he walked away.

When Father McDonough prayed over Rob and Kevin, Rob hit the floor like a ton of bricks. He was mortified. "How embarrassing is *that*?" he said, as his face turned bright red. Rob had just gone through something called "resting in the spirit" and while it isn't necessarily a sign of physical healing, it is a wonderful, peaceful experience. Rob and Kevin were then enlisted as "catchers" of other pilgrims, which they thought was a lot of fun.

As we were leaving the church, Nancy approached us and said, "I am so glad to see leaders of American families here in Medjugorje. We do not usually see men visiting alone." During our conversation, we heard a disturbance outside and Nancy rushed out to see what had happened. Father McDonough, who was not a young man, had taken a bad fall on the steps of the church. There was no ambulance nearby and he was losing a lot of blood. So Nancy fashioned a makeshift tourniquet from a scarf and enlisted us to carry him to her car for a trip to the hospital.

Nancy joined us in the waiting room and sat on one of the hard wooden benches. She was easy company. She said she lived in Medjugorje and since everyone here seemed to have a story, we asked how she had ended up there. Her husband Patrick had run a very successful car dealership in Canada and had been married and divorced several times before he met

Nancy. By his own admission he had a led shallow, materialistic existence and cared little for anyone but himself. Nancy owned a book of Our Lady's messages from Medjugorje which she kept on the table for her reflection. Patrick kept telling her to throw it out and she would reply, "No, you throw it out." But for some reason he never did. One day Patrick picked the book up and read, *"I am calling you to conversion for the last time."* He believed these words were meant for him. Leaving their lives and successful careers behind, they came to Medjugorje, where they built a large home for priests on retreat and for those discerning a priestly vocation. Nancy became a translator for Father Jozo. Patrick began hosting the hundreds of clergy members who flocked to their home for reflection and prayer. It later became a regular stop for tour groups who came to hear talks by Patrick and Nancy.

We were all inspired by this story, but it seemed that Our Lady had another reason for introducing us to Nancy. After talking about our families and our time in Medjugorje, she said, "You will never believe what happened to us this morning." Her friend, Marija, was the survivor of a botched abortion that her mother had attempted. Marija was born alive, and carried many physical and emotional scars. All she wanted in life was to become a nun but her disabilities made this nearly impossible. That day, however, after much politicking and persuasion, Marija was about to be accepted into a local order. Thrilled for her, Nancy wanted to find the perfect "engagement present for Marija's wedding to Jesus."

That morning, she and her husband had gone to Apparition Hill before sunrise to pray for guidance about the right gift. They prayed in pitch darkness at the summit and then went to meditate at the Blue Cross. As the sun came up, they saw Mary's sculptured hands holding the most beautiful golden rosary beads they had ever seen. Nancy believed the beads were intended for Marija, and getting this extraordinary gift brought her friend to tears.

We told Nancy that we had been at the Blue Cross the night before and had placed white plastic beads in Mary's hands. Since our arrival, people had been telling us about plastic and other materials turning to gold here. Could they have been the same beads we left? Nancy, accustomed to the things that happened in this sacred place, was ecstatic and felt sure that they were.

Father McDonough needed stitches, so it was a while before we left the hospital. When we finally got underway, Nancy reminded us that it was September 8 and suggested we sing "Happy Birthday" to Our Lady—something we would have found absolutely crazy back home. Suddenly an alarm went off in the car. Nancy kept her watch alarm set to 5:40 p.m., the time of Our Lady's daily apparitions. I looked up and saw the sun do something strange. It appeared to be dropping to the earth and then bouncing back to the sky. The same phenomenon, I would only learn later, had occurred before thousands of witnesses in Fatima on October 13, 1917.

I screamed "Stop the car!" and we all got out. I told Rob and Kevin to look at the sun and they both saw it spinning in the sky—another common experience in Medjugorje. Witnesses report that the interior of the sun is covered as happens during a solar eclipse, protecting the eye from damage, while the edges spin faster and faster, shooting off an array of astonishing colors. Millions have reportedly seen this happen. But what I saw was entirely different. And I would never forget it.

Kevin, Rob and Artie tour the walled city of Dubrovnik, the last stop on their trip.

11

Miracle on the Mountain

From the time I arrived in Medjugorje, I have felt filled with the light of Jesus. I feel like I have been healed physically and spiritually by this light. It reminds me of a childhood experience when I found a field mouse frozen in our backyard. I brought him into the sun and stroked him until he came to life and scampered away. I remember thinking how good God was to give us the sun to heal this little animal. God is truly light.

It was our last morning in Medjugorje, another sunny day with no wind and a temperature of 78 degrees. We were very fortunate because summers there can be extremely hot and oppressive—good for the crops, tough on the pilgrims. Our weather had been perfect.

I found myself only thinking of Christ and his mother. My sole desire was prayer. I knew this place had the same profound effect on many people. The three of us were reluctant to leave because we feared that we might lose our spiritual enthusiasm and revert to our old ways. But I knew our stopover in Dubrovnik would afford me some rest, and with my cancer surgery still scheduled for the next week, I needed it. It was time to go.

When we had climbed Cross Mountain two nights before, I had felt an intense pain in my lung. I really believed that I had been healed, so I called my wife to tell her I wanted another CT scan before I underwent surgery.

Not all doctors believe in miracles and my oncologist clearly did not. His office left a voicemail saying he knew where I was, and why I was there, but that "cancer doesn't just disappear" and I would still need the operation. So Judy found another doctor. Someone had mentioned a cancer specialist at MGH named Matthew Smith. Dr. Smith agreed to the new scan and scheduled it immediately after my return to Boston.

Zeljka came over to say goodbye and brought each of us a candle for our altars at home. I told her the story of the golden rosary beads and she was so moved that she cried, convinced that it was the work of Our Lady. She reached into her pocket and pulled out a set of rosary beads from Vicka which had been blessed during an apparition. She gave them to me.

Martin had arranged for a car to take us to Dubrovnik that afternoon, and we wanted to say goodbye to the Lattas before we left. Kevin had been longing to walk through the grape fields since we arrived, so we humored him and set off on foot. I had been trying to take it easy, and to rest when I could, but we had been driven around all week and the other guys craved a walk. We went slowly and agreed to take a cab back.

It was worth the trip. The rows of beautiful plump grapes were at least twice the size of those we saw at home, the healthiest looking fruits I'd ever seen. They glisten in the bright sunlight as if they have been dipped in sugar.

The native clay earth, dusty and orange, stuck to our shoes and pants. Along the way we saw vendors selling handmade local crafts. There were cars along the side of the path with merchandise displayed. It wasn't quite a flea market but it had that feel.

We met a wizened old woman selling altar cloths, with her hair in a tight white bun, her small dark eyes taking in the steady flow of foot traffic. She was stooped at the waist, but still managed to smile and greet the tourists. She told us that she had been injured in a fall when she was twenty-five and could never work, so she had supported herself for the last sixty years by making lace. We each purchased a beautiful cloth for our homes and she beamed her gratitude. We continued on our way.

When we entered the Latta's courtyard, Patrick dropped everything and rushed over to shake our hands and offer us tea and grapes. He was older than Nancy—perhaps in his mid-forties—with white hair, gold-rimmed glasses, and blue eyes. Patrick was very engaging, and it was easy to see why he had been so successful in the auto industry. But now he used his gifts for God's glory. Nancy had already told us about their conversion, but it appeared that there was more to the story.

Patrick told us about his two sons. He admitted that he had not been a good father, and that his kids had paid the price. At age fifteen, one was expelled from an expensive boarding school for using and distributing drugs. The other was a womanizer and drinker. Patrick prayed to the Blessed Mother to take his boys under her protection.

Both sons eventually visited Patrick in Medjugorje. After a trip to the Oasis of Peace, the place of Ray Baril's healing, the younger son experienced a conversion that eventually led him into the seminary, where he finished first in his class. The older son came to the Latta's home very reluctantly, warning his father that he didn't "believe in this stuff." Upon arrival, he headed downtown for a drink. His father, with total trust in the Blessed Mother, said, "Do what you please." Looking for a bar, the son found the St. James confessionals instead and decided to go in. I don't know what happened in there, but he hasn't taken a drink since, and is now a fireman in Vancouver who teaches teenagers about the dangers of drug and alcohol abuse.

Nancy came out and her face lit up as she said, "Praise God you are here!" She sat in the courtyard with us as we spoke of many things—of yesterday's car ride, Father McDonough, and my upcoming cancer surgery.

We formed such a wonderful friendship with the Lattas that we wanted to keep in touch. Nancy began to write their address for us, then suddenly dropped her head in prayer—something we had become accustomed to on this trip. We also bowed our own heads and sat quietly, waiting for her to speak. When she did, she looked directly at me and said, "We can never be truly free until we forgive." I had already been to Confession. Twice. And I believed that I'd forgiven everyone I needed to. Puzzled, I wondered how her words might apply to me, and came up empty. So Nancy said, "You need to forgive your mother and father."

That hit me like a ton of bricks. My parents had just divorced after forty-three years of marriage. It was eating me up inside, and I didn't even realize it. I began to cry in deep wracking sobs, and Nancy held my head in her hands. Rob and Kevin, who had parent issues of their own, were weeping as well. It was a very powerful moment: three grown men crying cleansing tears in a courtyard in Bosnia.

After this week's waterworks, it was another miracle that we weren't dehydrated. We had packed our own food and water but should have considered packing Kleenex and Gatorade instead.

Nancy asked the date of my surgery and when I answered, "September 14," she immediately exclaimed, "That's the Feast of the Triumph of the Cross! You will be fine!"

As we were leaving, the Lattas invited us to return with our families. We said that we hoped to, and we really meant it.

We hurried back to the house to meet our ride to Dubrovnik. The Cilics were there to say goodbye, along with some other new friends from the pilgrimage. While it was nowhere near as tearful as our sendoff had been in Hingham five days ago, there was a certain symmetry. We felt like we were leaving another family here.

The ride to our next destination was very scenic, taking us through the mountains of Croatia. The view was only marred by the same kind of war damage we had experienced on our way to Medjugorje.

We finally reached the Adriatic Sea. The vistas were incredible and the air and water pristine. But then we came upon the charred remains of an enormous fire that had consumed millions of acres of trees. The hillsides were black, a stark contrast to the shimmering green water below.

Finally we saw Dubrovnik jutting out into the water, surrounded by a seventy-five-foot stone wall. The sea ends where the wall begins and we could see the limestone mountains rising up behind it. Dubrovnik deserves its title, "Pearl of the Adriatic."

Our driver left us with our guide, Sylvia. She told us that the massive walls had been built between the eleventh and seventeenth centuries to protect a major trading port. Dubrovnik still looks very medieval. We saw palaces, monasteries, and centuries-old houses nestled along narrow streets. There are thirty churches within the walls of the city. As we walked the cobbled streets, Sylvia pointed out the damage from the recent Serbian-Croatian war. Large portions of the wall and more than two-thirds of the buildings had been hit, and fires had destroyed many historic structures.

Despite the damage, the city was absolutely stunning. Our visit served as a nice transition from Medjugorje to the "real world," but after my experience with Our Lady, it was somewhat anticlimactic. I had too much on my mind to fully appreciate architecture.

We spent the night at the Hotel Lero, ending our day with more journal work. Kevin summed it up best when he wrote, "This has been an amazing journey. I am sure that the bond created among the three of us is one that we will hold dearly for the rest of our lives. We shared. We cried. And we grew." Exhausted, we said a Peace Rosary and went to sleep. In the morning we departed for home. We couldn't wait to see our families and share the gift of Medjugorje with all of them. Of course, I was anxious to learn the results of my new CT scan in the days to come. Had I truly been healed?

Family Trip to Medjugorje, June, 2001, on stairs of Virgin Mary Assumption Church, Siroki Brijeg.
Top Row: (Left to Right): Father Jozo Zovko, Kathy Griffin, Janice Clunan, Jack O'Donaghue, Mike O'Donaghue, Lisa O'Donaghue, Rita Gill, Kathryn Boyle, Artie Boyle, Judy Boyle, Brendan Boyle, Rob Griffin, Kevin Gill.
Second Row: Artie Boyle, Jr., Christopher Boyle, Jack Greeley, Corey Griffin, Kevin Gill, Jr., Patrick Gill, Marianne Gill.
First Row: Stephanie Gill, Christine Gill, Gabrielle Boyle, Julianne Boyle, Casey Griffin, Tim Boyle, Jack O'Donaghue, Jr., Mike Griffin.

12

Homecoming

On the day that I had been scheduled to have my lung removed, I was on the golf course instead. I felt different in every way. Not only had Jesus restored my physical health, he had given me peace of mind, and a complete spiritual transformation.

On our flight home, I thought about all that had happened since we left Boston. There was too much to process, but I was greatly uplifted by the pilgrimage, and by the privilege I'd had of sharing it with friends. We weren't just three guys on a plane, but three men on the journey of a lifetime.

At last we landed in Boston. Our wives were waiting at the airport and we were absolutely overjoyed to see them. We could not wait to tell them about what had happened, but they could all see that something was new. It was in our faces and in our voices. We were simply not the same men.

As I'd requested, when we arrived home my entire family was present. In front of everyone there, I brought my father forward and told him that I forgave him for divorcing my mother. My mother didn't like it, but she knew it was something I had to do.

I knew that I had experienced a spiritual healing. Of that there was no question. But what about the cancer? I'd had a glimpse of heaven, but I still didn't want to die.

With difficulty, Judy had managed to get another CT scan scheduled two days before the planned surgery, but I still had to follow through with pre-admission and pre-op tests, including one to evaluate pulmonary function. At 11:30 a.m. on September 12, the technician performed the respiratory test. He got a puzzled look on his face and asked, "What are you doing here?" That raised my hopes, but I kept myself in check and waited for the results. I drove to the lab in Chelsea to pick up the films and bring them to my doctor's office at the hospital.

I rushed to the thoracic surgeon's office and he met me at the door. He looked at the scans, scratched his chin, and said the two words that every cancer patient prays for: "They're gone." He informed me that the large aggressive tumor had disappeared and that the two smaller ones had shrunk to an insignificant size.

On the day that I had been scheduled to have my lung removed, I was on the golf course instead. I felt different in every way. Not only had Jesus restored my physical health, he had given me peace of mind, and a complete spiritual transformation. This time I wouldn't forget it.

To my surprise, as I moved around the course, I realized that for the first time I was unconcerned about the score. I wanted to win, of course. I always would. But I heard myself complimenting other players on a long drive or a skillful putt and began to realize that their success did not diminish my own.

All my sporting life, I couldn't have cared less about my opponents, as long as I kicked their butts. But now my competitive nastiness was gone—not just from my golf game, but from my experience of hockey, business, and even my kids' sports activities.

I recognized that God controls my life, and that on the whole, I do not. In Medjugorje, I came to terms with losing my life. At the top of Cross Mountain following

Confession, I was no longer afraid of dying. If I could surrender to my mortality, life's greatest adversary, what else really mattered? No matter how hard I tried, I couldn't beat cancer. I didn't triumph. God did. It's the same with everything else.

I learned that life is far less stressful when we accept that we are not in charge. It doesn't all depend on us. We have to manage our lives to the best of our abilities, to love God, our families, and our friends. But we don't hold the power.

This second time around, I had been healed spiritually as well as physically, and would do everything I could to maintain my strong relationship with God and to share it with my family. Ten months after our return, Kevin, Rob, and I visited Medjugorje with our families—all twenty-seven of us—and shared with them the beauty and wonder of this special place.

Artie and Ivan inside St. James Church.

13

The Fruits of Faith

Following my pilgrimage, my wife and I introduced more prayer into the Boyle household. We had always worshipped as a family in church, but now began doing more at home, with me often leading a family Rosary. We spoke about Jesus and Mary, and tried our best to incorporate faith into every aspect of lives, even sports.

When we landed at Logan Airport on September 10, 2000, we thought we had completed our journey, but the changes in our lives had only begun. Our wives were amazed by how the trip had affected us.

The first time I was healed in 1999, I didn't do anything differently. This time, I promised to show my gratitude by encouraging devotion to the Rosary, and witnessing to the love and intercession of Our Lady wherever possible. My wife and I introduced more prayer into the Boyle household. We had always worshipped as a family in church, but now began doing more at home, with me often leading a family Rosary. We spoke about Jesus and Mary, and tried our best to incorporate faith into every aspect of our lives, even sports. When Judy and I began our prayer group, the kids would attend weekly, and observe people devoted to their faith. This made them more comfortable praying in front of others.

Both Kevin and Rob shared the messages of Our Lady with their families.

At Rob's house, he and Cathy spoke more about God with their children, beginning each day with a holy water blessing and ending it with a family prayer. Rob said that even as teenagers his children kept up the habit of prayer. Daily prayer helped them find their moral compass and keep their faith.

Rob now attends Mass almost every day, and faithfully recites his daily Rosary.

Rob finds that receiving Jesus every day helps him to stay on track. So does Confession. Since his reconciliation with Father Simon in Medjugorje, Rob confesses his sins promptly and candidly. Every day he recites the verse: "I am an unprofitable servant; I have done what I was obliged to do." (Lk 17:5-1) The result of all this striving and prayer is that he cares more about others both in his personal life and in his everyday business dealings.

Rob's industry, commercial real estate, is highly competitive and so is Rob. But now he recognizes competitiveness as a potentially destructive force. Before his conversion, he used to see business as a "zero-sum game." Now Rob views profits as a reflection of God's abundance. There's plenty of good to go around for everyone, and there's no excuse for hoarding it. He has tried to change his company's organizational culture from one of "superstars" to that of a cohesive team. His shift away from hyper-competitiveness extends beyond the office. For example, Rob says he now plays golf for the pure pleasure of it, rather than as an opportunity to "crush" the competition.

Rob is not afraid to speak openly about his faith, even at work. He tells his employees that it is the cornerstone of his success. Even with non-Catholics, Rob acknowledges his religion. But he doesn't marginalize others' beliefs, because he knows that there is only one God, one Mediator.

Rob emphasizes the importance of setting goals in all areas of life—and remembering to ask for God's help in achieving them. "Ask and you shall receive, seek and you shall find," (Mt. 7:7) is a verse that we learned in Medjugorje to treat almost as mantra.

Like all of us, he admits to having flaws. He wakes up every morning and tells God, "I'm sorry. I apologize for my faults. Please guide me and let me know your will." He says that he needs to "put on the armor every day," because the closer you get to God, the more difficult the Evil One makes things for you. He knows our most vulnerable area, whether it's our children, our marriages, our finances, or whatever else matters most to us.

Rob finds that when things are going too well, he gets complacent. So he uses holy water and holy oil daily to remind him of his need for God's protection. Medjugorje was life-changing for him. He wants to be sure he stays "on fire."

Kevin was changed as well. To understand his transformation, you need to understand what he was like before. He had been raised Catholic, and just "went with the flow," practicing the faith out of deference to his parents. He suspected that God existed, but only turned to him in hard times, of which he said there weren't that many. Then I got sick and he began to pray in earnest.

Kevin left for Medjugorje with specific goals in mind, such as memorizing all the mysteries of the

Rosary. But when we arrived, he went with the flow in an entirely different way, allowing himself to be led. After what happened there, he had a concrete experience of the reality of God, and knew that he had to get himself in line, by living the messages that we had learned there. (Remember the five stones? Prayer, bible-reading, fasting, Confession, and the Eucharist.)

Going to Confession had an enormous impact on Kevin, helping him realize for the first time that he was broken, too. He had a wonderful marriage and family, but there was something within needing repair. He said it felt as if Father Simon had reached inside and changed his heart.

Today, Kevin wears his religion on his sleeve. Before our trip, when his wife hung Rosary beads on the car visor, he removed them so he wouldn't offend potential clients. Now he realized that this had been a cop-out, and proudly put the Rosary back where it belonged. Like Rob, he now speaks openly about his beliefs at work, and has a reputation in the industry as being very spiritual. That's fine with him. His openness hasn't hurt his business.

In addition to family Rosary at Kevin's house, Rita and Judy began a weekly children's Rosary, welcoming everyone from infants to teens. They've watched children go from barely grasping the beads to helping others learn the prayers. We have all encouraged our kids to make use of the sacraments more, and we lead by example. Sometimes we do really well. Other times we find ourselves slipping a little. But that's life. We get back up and try harder, ironically finding that the solution is the very sacraments we've been neglecting.

Shortly after returning from Medjugorje, I attended an event at St. John's Church in Quincy, Massachusetts. I had not yet met Ivan, one of the six visionaries, but he would be present at the service, to which I was bringing a sick friend. We sat as close to the front as possible.

The evening began with the Rosary. At 6:40 p.m. (the time Our Lady comes to him each day), Ivan left the front pew and walked to the altar. The church was completely still. He knelt with his back to us and began to speak with her. No one could hear the conversation; his lips moved but there was no sound. As Ivan walked down from the altar that night, he looked at me and winked. At first I thought I must have imagined it, but then was sure I hadn't. Why would he do that?

After the Rosary and Mass, Ivan gave a talk. He said that Our Lady had blessed everyone present, especially the sick and priests, and all our religious articles. She said that she would recommend all of us to her son.

Through a translator, Ivan talked about the first days of the apparitions, admitting that he had been very frightened at the time. He spoke about Our Lady's beauty, saying that if we could see her for just one second, we would quickly lose interest in the things of this world. He recounted asking her on one occasion, "Why are you so beautiful?" and her reply, "Because I love." Ivan said that he had asked the Blessed Mother why she chose him. She answered, "I do not always choose the best." Rather, she said, she picks people who will "get the job done." She also advised us to pray for three hours every day.

After his talk, Ivan came up behind me, tapped my shoulder, looked at me, and then just walked away. Now I knew that I hadn't imagined the wink. Seeing that he was about to leave, I followed him. I had so many things I wanted to ask: What it was like to see the Blessed Mother? To live under Communism? Was my deceased son, Joseph, okay? Finally, I wanted to know *why*. Why had I been healed? What did God want from me?

Carol Cohoon, the event coordinator, was escorting Ivan out. I asked if I could take him to dinner. Carol quickly said, "No, Ivan doesn't do that." I really wanted my questions answered, and to know why he'd acted as though he knew me. I was disappointed not to meet him, but it had been a great evening anyway.

Meanwhile, the media interest in my story continued, and on Christmas Eve 2000 Judy and I appeared on the front page of *The Boston Globe* in an article called, "It's a Wonderful Life." The reporter, who happened to be Jewish, was fascinated by the story and did a great job telling it.

Unbeknownst to me, Ivan read the story, and he left a message on our answering machine saying that he'd like to meet me. I took Ivan out for dinner and got the chance to ask my questions. Not all of them were answered. He said he didn't know about Joseph; he only knew what Our Lady chose to tell him. When I inquired why he'd approached me at St. John's that night, he gave a little smile and wouldn't answer. I've never been able to get that out of him.

We became fast friends. Ivan invited me to speak at apparitions, and give witness to my healing through the intercession of the Blessed Mother. In the beginning I brought notes, but Ivan laughed at me, and I soon began speaking from the heart.

In January 2001 Judy and I were invited to Ivan's home to witness his apparition in private. He and his wife lived in a small second floor apartment on Prince Street in Boston's historic North End. The place was so small there was barely room for the four of us. It was thrilling to be so near him as he spoke with the Blessed Mother, and Judy and I felt incredibly privileged.

In January 2001, Judy and I began a weekly Rosary group at our house. (The crowd would become so large that we soon had to relocate to St. Paul's Church downtown.) In February, Ivan suggested that I host him at my home during an apparition. The whole thing felt surreal. We were awestruck that Our Lady would be visiting us. It was an honor and a gift, and we made sure all of the kids were present.

Judy and I decided not to issue invitations or limit attendance, thinking that the Blessed Mother would determine who should be there. Word spread like wildfire and people from everywhere wanted to come.

The phone was ringing off the hook; a woman whose brother was seriously ill called to ask if they could park an ambulance in the driveway; others inquired about bringing children, or extending the invitation to friends; our parish called to warn us not to claim that Mary was appearing at our home. It was bedlam.

I felt that things were getting out of control, that we would be overrun, that the neighbors would hate us, and that the police would arrive. But Judy insisted that Our Lady would keep things from becoming too crazy. And so she did. Despite the crowds, the house was fine, the neighbors weren't disturbed, and there were no patrol cars.

Hundreds of people from all walks of life appeared on our doorstep—mostly believers, but a handful of skeptics too. Ivan sat to await his apparition on the deck because there was more room for people outside. You could suddenly smell roses in our kitchen—but there were no roses present. This is a phenomenon that the Church calls "the odor of sanctity."

Our son, Brendan came home, and saw the ambulance in the driveway. He raced into the kitchen, frightened, only to find three of the NHL's toughest players kneeling on the floor. They have all since experienced conversions.

Ivan began having monthly apparitions in our living room, and we invited the Gills and the Griffins to participate. These regular gatherings kept everyone connected and helped us to continue what we began in Medjugorje. It made the kids conscious of the tremendous gifts we'd received, and made them eager to share the message.

While he's a holy man, Ivan is also a regular guy. He and I began attending sporting events and playing golf together. Over the years, he, his wife, Laureen, and their children have become very dear friends of ours.

Gill Family in Medjugorje, Apparition Hill, June 2001.
Back row: Marianne, Kevin, Stephanie, Rita, Kevin Jr.
Front row: Christine and Patrick. Elizabeth Gill (not pictured) would be born in 2004.

Griffin Family in Medjugorje, Apparition Hill, June 2001.
Back row: Corey, Rob, Cathy.
Front row: Mike and Casey.

14

The Message Goes Viral

When we formed the prayer group in 2001, we dedicated it to Our Lady of Medjugorje. The graces received, the prayers answered, and the miracles witnessed are vivid proof to us of her intervention and of the generous response of her son.

As news of my healing spread, we received more and more media requests. Following our family's appearance on *The Early Show*, which brought a film crew to capture "a day in the life of the Boyles," there were segments on *20/20*, *Nightline*, and *Good Morning America*. For me, a kid born in the projects, it was pretty overwhelming. But I knew this wasn't about me; it was about witnessing to my healing through the intercession of Mary.

We had talked about returning to Medjugorje with our families and so we did in June 2001. The logistics of traveling with twenty-seven people were pretty complicated, but it all came together very quickly. In addition to the Gills and the Griffins, we invited Jackie O'Donaghue and his family because it was his healing that had brought us there in the first place.

It was a long trip with many layovers, and with nineteen kids ranging in age from five to eighteen, we worried how they would act on arrival. But from the time we landed, it was as if the world had turned upside down. Our children were actually fighting over who would lead the prayers. They got up early every morning; ran to save seats at Mass, Rosary and Adoration; and spent their own money on rosary beads and medals. One day several of them arose at dawn to climb Cross Mountain with Jackie O'Donaghue. When we developed the pictures at home, there were some very unusual effects, including really odd lights and colors, and images that resembled angels and St.

Padre Pio. We visited the Lattas again, and met with Father Jozo in his private chapel—a rare opportunity for our kids to meet someone who had been persecuted for the Faith. It was an unforgettable week.

In the summer of 2002, I organized an "Eight Man Trip" where Rob, Kevin and I brought some of our friends to see the place of my healing, and to visit with Ivan. Father Simon joined us there, too. It was especially powerful for the first-time visitors, many of whom were profoundly changed. One of them, Garry Hebert, a gifted singer, found himself on the altar singing the hymns during Mass. When he went home, he became a Catholic.

In summer 2004 I planned a "Forty Man Trip," which included my sons Brendan and Brian. It was important for me to share this experience with men. From the time I was healed, Our Lady pressed upon my heart that men, in particular, really need to pray. They are the head of the family while their wives are the heart. If the men set an example of prayer, the children will imitate them. That creates peace in the family, which leads to peace in the world.

Since my miracle, I have been invited to speak around the world. The most memorable trips have been those I've taken with Ivan. We have traveled to Europe, South America, Canada, and all over the United States. More than a decade later, being with Ivan during his apparitions still lifts my spirit and touches my soul.

On one trip to Ireland Ivan and I made several stops. We first visited Galway City, and Taughmaconnell, County Roscommon, but the largest crowd by far was in Clonfort, a small rural area in East County Galway. Six thousand people started arriving at 8 a.m. for the evening service. Mass was in the main hall, but there were four other buildings with closed circuit television for the overflow crowd. The congregation was fervently singing the hymns of St. James Cathedral. We weren't too surprised; at the time, the Irish ranked second to Americans as Medjugorje pilgrims.

Of all the places Ivan and I have journeyed, none would affect us more than our trip to the Peruvian slums. When we met Father Simon Cadwallader in the confessionals, he had been stationed in England. He was later moved to the missions in Lima, Peru.

After a brief stopover to visit a parish in La Paz, Bolivia, we traveled to Via El Salvador, Peru, the first "planned shantytown" in the world. There were a million people and nearly as many dogs—vicious, ugly, scary dogs. They were very threatening and your only protection was to throw dirt at them. The people on the streets looked dangerous, too.

The shanties were wide open, made from tin, newspapers and cardboard. All the food was exposed and covered with flies. The only water source was a series of fifty-five gallon drums in the street, which were only refreshed once a week, and were used by the people for cooking, bathing, and drinking.

That night, we spoke at Father Simon's Mass at the hilltop church. Outside there were many little street lights in the darkness, and the effect was actually beautiful. But then the sun came up and you could once again see the ugliness.

Over the years, Father Simon became a member of our families. Since his Peruvian mission, Father Simon has spent time off at the Gills' and the Griffins', and when possible, his father, Bill, joins him from England. Via El Salvador is a tough assignment but Simon is truly a committed servant of God.

My talks have yielded another fruit—more pilgrimages to Medjugorje, some of them "buddy journeys" like my own. Chuck Bean has multiple sclerosis and heard of my healing from a hometown friend. When Father Simon was visiting Hingham, Chuck attended a healing Mass, followed by my talk. A month later, at Red Sox Opening Day, he and his friends were inspired to plan a men's Medjugorje trip modeled on our own. Once again, Our Lady reached out to men where they congregated.

The men's trip made a deep impact on each of them. They spent time with Ivan attending apparitions in his private chapel. They were awe-struck as they climbed Apparition Hill and Cross Mountain. They recited more Rosaries at Medjugorje than they had in their entire lives. And like us, they decided to return with their wives and children.

After his pilgrimage, Chuck believes he is a better husband, father, friend, and co-worker. His MS has stopped progressing and he's no longer taking medication.

When we formed the prayer group in 2001, we dedicated it to Our Lady of Medjugorje. The graces received, the prayers answered, and the miracles witnessed are vivid proof to us of her intervention and of the generous response of her son.

One of the most remarkable events was the healing of a little girl named Grace. Emily and Jim Elliot had been married for ten years and had two boys—Jake, seven, and Matthew, five. Emily wanted another baby, but she didn't think it was possible. She had a devotion to the Rosary following a Medjugorje pilgrimage. The couple prayed and agreed to trust God's plan for their family. Emily also prayed to St. Therese the Little Flower, secretly asking for yellow roses as a sign. Jim, who rarely brought flowers, suddenly presented two dozen yellow roses to his wife.

Grace Therese Elliot was born October 1, the Feast of St. Therese. Her parents were overjoyed, until the doctors announced that Grace had a serious medical problem: her urinary ducts were located outside the bladder, causing potentially dangerous infections.

So Emily brought Grace to our prayer group, to join Ivan for his apparition. Sitting among the 200 people filling our home, Grace was calm for 40 minutes during the Rosary. But just as Ivan knelt before Our Lady, she began screaming. Emily was mortified but was trapped in the crowd and couldn't take her outside. Grace cried through the entire apparition. The moment it ended, she stopped. People wondered aloud whether this meant she had enjoyed a healing—or at least the beginning of one.

Still contemplating the risky surgery that doctors had said that Grace would require, her parents brought her to a healing service with Father Tom DiLorenzo, a priest who had prayed with me. Father Tom, who hadn't been told anything about Grace, held her and asked, "What's happening with her bladder?" Emily briefed him. He said, "This child has already been healed by God." The Elliotts hoped that he was right, but they continued to pray as a family for her recovery.

Shortly thereafter, they took Grace to the specialist to be retested. He announced, to his own surprise, that the problem ducts had physically moved back inside the bladder and everything was normal. The surgery was cancelled. As of this writing, Grace is a healthy ten year-old, with two younger siblings.

Jack Creehan was twenty-seven years old and in great physical condition. In fact, he was a competitive runner. But one day as he took part in a road race, he suddenly collapsed. The paramedics "coded" him (pronounced him dead) four separate times and it seemed impossible that he would survive. Even if he did revive, doctors predicted permanent brain damage. We invited the family to our prayer group at St. Paul's Church, and arranged for a Mass to be said for him that evening. His entire family came and we prayed over them, and over a large picture of him placed near the altar. Many of his friends arrived to fill the lower level of the church. The next day, his family learned from doctors that he had made a complete recovery.

Dr. Jon Gallen worked as an anesthesiologist in Brockton, Massachusetts, and lived in our neighborhood. We became friends because our kids played hockey with his kids. He had developed the rare, fatal blood cancer called multiple myeloma and was already very ill. His doctors offered little hope. He was already wasting away to nothing. The bony tumors this disease generates had spread so far in his body that it was too painful for him to sit. He came to our prayer group as a last resort, not knowing how a bunch of Catholics would respond to a Jewish doctor. However, when we welcomed him and brought him to the front of the church to be prayed over, he couldn't believe the love and outpouring of support. Judy gave him Rosary beads and a small container of holy water. He left uplifted and went home. He spread the holy water all over himself, leaving half the bottle remaining, and went to sleep. The next morning he awoke to find the bottle filled and called out to his wife—asking why she'd meddled with his holy water bottle. She said, "I never touched it."

Soon after, Jon began to get well. The tumors disappeared. Still proudly Jewish, he began to attend our Rosary meetings, wearing his beads around his neck—until someone gently explained that you're not supposed to do that! Jon is still free of the disease, and lives now in California.

The blessings have continued to come. I remember the woman who ran a working farm in our town, whom everyone called "Mrs. R." One day in church, Mrs. R came up to Rose, a member of our prayer group, and begged her to pray for her daughter. That young girl had just been diagnosed with a malignant tumor on her ovaries. The next day they were headed to Dana Farber Cancer Center, for doctors to mark her body for the risky, essential surgery. Rose headed straight for our Rosary group, and believing that children's prayers are more powerful, had her own daughters add Mrs. R's intention that night. The next day, the doctors found that the tumor had completely disappeared. It has never returned.

There have been many other prayers answered—some of them not in the way that we had hoped.

In the beginning, Judy and I felt our role was to pray with people so they would get well. We have since realized that sometimes we are supposed to help escort people to heaven. Over the years we have had to say goodbye to many people. Donnie Higgins, thirty-two, had a wife and four young children. Fighting cancer, he attended our Rosary group for two years before starting his own weekly prayer group at Gate of Heaven Church, South Boston. Although he died, his father now leads it and people come faithfully.

Little eight-year-old Marisol Liliana O'Brien died of a disease called leukodystrophy, which had already stolen her ability to walk and talk. Yet in the five years she came to St. Paul's on Thursday evenings, she brought joy to everyone she met. We also loved five-year-old Calle Cronk, baby Charlotte, and others who went home to God. We still miss them.

People sometimes think Judy and I have a formula for healing or a better connection to God than they do. We don't. All we can tell them is that when I was ill, what I believe God wanted from me was to have faith; to seek and offer forgiveness; and to surrender everything to him. That is very hard to do when you or a loved one are facing a serious sickness or disability.

I also sought the intercession of the Blessed Mother. Many people ask why we pray to her instead of directly to Jesus. Judy puts it beautifully. She says that Mary purifies our prayers before taking them to her Son. She removes any of the pride, or envy, or anger or other negative things attached to them. It's like buying a new dress shirt. Before wearing it, you take out the pins and the cardboard, then launder and press the shirt to get it ready. Our Mother does this with our requests, and as Ivan tells us after apparitions, she recommends us and our needs to her Son.

Father Ed McDonough used to explain it this way: God surely wants us to be well, and sometimes that's what happens. But his primary goal is our salvation. So he begins with the things that threaten us spiritually.

The most important thing is our spiritual health. If we do not have this, we cannot possibly enter God's Kingdom. Second is a healing from mental illness, which can also keep us from God. Physical healing comes after these two because illness and pain rarely keep us from heaven. In fact, quite the contrary. Many of the saints were given sickness and suffering to prepare them for what God wanted them to do.

However, we should always ask the Father for what we want. St. Bernard Clairvaux used to say, "Ask much of God and you will receive much. Ask little and you will receive little." All we can do is pray and trust.

Before my illness and healing in Medjugorje, I was always in a hurry, entirely focused on tasks. Now, I stop and smell the roses—quite literally. I actually take time to appreciate God's flowers, and even put a rose tree at my front door so that I can enjoy their beauty every day. This bush bursts forth beautiful blooms all spring, summer and fall.

I love our neighborhood because it manifests the Creator's handiwork in beautiful sunsets and sunrises, in abundant wildlife such as the turkeys, hawks, foxes, deer and other critters who pass through our neck of the woods. I was fascinated with nature as a child, but forgot it in the press of work and family. That youthful appreciation returned along with my health.

I no longer worry as much. I tend to pray and let God handle whatever it is that is vexing me. My new job is a good example. I got sick of the trucking industry and left it to enter the mortgage business—just in time for the 2008 banking crisis that crashed the U.S. economy. I didn't agonize about that. Instead, I just plugged along and prayed that God would allow me to work in the Church yet still manage to support my family. I'm now a development officer at the Archdiocese of Boston, working with priests and volunteers, as well as speaking to CCD and youth groups.

I feel like every day has 25 hours in it. I stop to sit and talk with people and actually listen. I find them fascinating and realize that we all have a story. I love giving talks because that always brings back the moment that I was healed, and I feel the power and the gratitude all over again.

I truly appreciate every single day, and if it happens to be a day of back pain, I offer it up in union with Jesus' sufferings, and welcome the pain as a reminder that I'm still alive. I realize that I could have died fourteen years ago, and contemplate all I that would have missed. I'm not sure if my destination then would have been heaven, hell, or purgatory. I do know that being here for the past fourteen years has been an amazing gift. I have seen graduations, weddings, the births of many grandchildren, and had the great pleasure of witnessing a son enter the seminary. And I've had all that extra time to enjoy with my lovely wife. I have learned a truer, deeper form of gratitude.

I have lived on a golf course, visited Hawaii three times, and am planning a fourth trip. I've met a visionary, been in the presence of the Blessed Mother countless times, and had a private audience with Pope John Paul II.

Although my hair is graying and thinning, I hope to age gracefully, with great appreciation for what God has given me and my family.

I try to live the Blessed Mother's messages but I'm not perfect. If I'm not careful, I find myself reverting to my old ways. I have to pray and stay vigilant to do what God asks of me. My weekly prayer group, and Ivan's prayer group, really help me.

As for my medical situation, the large aggressive tumor completely disappeared in Medjugorje and never came back. According to my doctors, the second set of CT scans showed that the two smaller ones had shrunk to an insignificant size. I feared surgery and so I let them sit for more than a year, by which point the technology had improved and the doctors could remove them laparoscopically without sawing through my ribs. Still nervous about the procedure, I prayed with Father Simon and Ivan, and Ivan promised me Our Lady would be in the operating room, and that Jesus' hands would guide the surgeon's. It went well. The tumors were in fact renal cells, but they had not grown or spread. With metastatic renal cell carcinoma this is virtually unheard of. I had been protected yet again. It is possible that I never needed the surgery at all, but my having the procedure gave everyone peace of mind. In 2000 Dr. McGovern said on CBS that absent a miracle, the cancer would return. Well, it hasn't. These many years later he says, "Every time I see you, I know God exists."

After a few years, my doctor and I agreed that I no longer needed follow-up scans. He told me, "You have graduated from the School of Oncology, something that very rarely happens."

Why didn't Jesus destroy the smaller tumors in Medjugorje rather than just shrinking them? I wish I knew. Maybe I needed more spiritual work first, or had to learn the lesson of perseverance. I don't know. I can't explain it any more than I can explain the miracle I had already received.

It's hard to believe that it has been fourteen years since my miraculous healing and that I still remain in perfect health. My first cure didn't change my life. The second one turned it upside down—or rather, right side up. Now I give witness to the healing power of God wherever and whenever I am asked. Doing this has not always been easy, but I know this is what God asks of me—as I'm reminded whenever I read the bible narrative of the ten lepers:

And it came to pass, as he was going to Jerusalem, he passed through the midst of Samaria and

Galilee. And as he entered into a certain town, there met him ten men that were lepers, who stood afar off; and lifted up their voice, saying: "Jesus, master, have mercy on us."

Whom when he saw, he said: "Go, shew yourselves to the priests." And it came to pass, as they went, they were made clean.

And one of them, when he saw that he was made clean, went back, with a loud voice glorifying God. And he fell on his face before his feet, giving thanks: and this was a Samaritan.

And Jesus answering, said, Were not ten made clean? and where are the nine? (Lk 17: 11-17)

Our 2000 pilgrimage transformed my life in every way. However, what I am most grateful for is the gift of life which I received on that mountain in Medjugorje.

Judy and Artie Boyle, 2014.

Acknowledgements

I want to thank first and foremost my wife and life partner, Judy. Our Lady tells us that the mother is the heart of the home, and no one depicts this better than Judy. Her relentless prayer and sacrifice has provided this family with love, kindness, and a spiritual presence through her prayer. Judy's unfailing faith that Our Lady's intersession through Jesus will pull us through any situation, regardless of how hopeless, has proven be true time and again. Her love and prayers have guided us in dealing with autism, the death of a child, job loss, and cancer. A fantastic cook who keeps a meticulous home (not an easy task with our clan), she is still beautiful after forty years of marriage. I am forever in thanks and in love.

All of our children have brought us great joy. From the eldest to the youngest, we have been graced with thirteen lights from heaven.

Jennifer is the oldest and a doctor; she was a successful student athlete at MIT in Cambridge before moving on to medical school, where she met her husband, Allan. They have eight terrific children. Jen was very helpful during my illness and continues to aid our large extended family.

Artie, Jr., who was born autistic, has brought us great joy through his love, kindness, and his victories in the Special Olympics, where almost all of his siblings have either taught or volunteered.

The third in line, Michelle, became a student athlete like her sister. Michelle stood out in track and field at Amherst College, where she met her husband, Eric. Michelle and Eric also have eight wonderful children. Both are very successful in business—Eric in finance and Michelle in real estate.

Christopher John spent ten years teaching theology at a Catholic high school in Boston after graduating from St. Joseph's College in Maine. Chris was a successful coach in baseball and football but excelled as the varsity swim coach. He has been a tremendous mentor for his younger brothers, who followed him to the school where he taught. His shining moment was when he entered the seminary this past September.

Number five, Brendan is an extremely versatile athlete, a gifted gymnast and diver—he was a four-time all-American diver at Connecticut College. He currently works in retail in the Boston area.

Kathryn followed Chris's footsteps into teaching. She graduated from St. Anselm's in New Hampshire, then taught theology at a Boston Catholic high school. She now directs the youth ministry program at St. Joseph's Parish in Holbrook, where she is much loved for her bigness of heart.

Seventh in line was Brian, who grew to be 6' 7"—four inches taller than any of his siblings. He was also gifted in athletics, especially hockey. He played at Boston College and was chosen in the first round of the NHL draft in 2003. He now plays for the New York Rangers.

Joseph Anthony followed Brian, but his life on this earth was cut short by Sudden Infant Death Syndrome. We were devastated, but time and prayer have shown us how to appreciate what time we had with him and what a great gift life is.

Judy thought that because our children had witnessed the death of Joseph that they should see the birth of our next child. She invited all seven children into the delivery room to watch Julianne come into this world. It was an amazing experience. Once she learned to talk, Julianne was precocious in a lovely way. She was sitting in the back of the church one day when a woman approached and asked who she was. She answered,

"I'm the glory of God"—that was something her mom had always told her. Julianne played basketball in high school and now attends Boston College.

Gabrielle we have nick-named "Blue Eyes," since she is the only sibling with that feature. Her dream is to write music and sing music, and she does both very well. We love to sit around listening to her strumming along and singing; the grandchildren think she's a superstar. Gabrielle graduated from Endicott College in Massachusetts, where she played lacrosse for four years.

Timothy is a gifted athlete who specializes in hockey. Tim was drafted in 2011 by the Ottawa Senators of the NHL. Tim is also the best golfer in the family at scratch but is closely pursued by his other brothers. Tim was part of the State Championship Catholic Memorial hockey team before finishing high school at Noble and Greenough in Dedham, Massachusetts.

Nicholas, a passionate and determined child, went to the same schools as Tim, and also plays on the hockey and golf teams. Nick has gone on service trips to Rome and down south, and he went to Medjugorje with Christopher and me and seventeen other boys from Catholic Memorial. A low handicap golfer, he hopes to pursue that sport in college.

Andrew, the baby of the family, also came along to Croatia. Andrew has a very big heart. He is easygoing and a pleasure to be around. He is a gifted golfer, captaining his high school team as a sophomore. He plays baseball and hockey as well, always trying to keep up with his brothers.

Each of our children is a great gift to us from God, and so we have consecrated each of them to the Immaculate Heart of Mary and the Sacred Heart of Jesus. It is our hope and prayer that they keep the faith, and that one day we will all be one big happy family in heaven.

I'd like to thank my Mom and Dad for their unyielding love and support during my time of need. I have been blessed with wonderful parents and will always treasure them both.

About the Authors

Arthur P. Boyle has traveled the world speaking to thousands of people in North and South America and Europe since his miraculous healing from cancer in Medjugorje in 2000. He is currently employed as a development officer for the Archdiocese of Boston. He and his wife Judy have thirteen children. He lives in Hingham, Massachusetts.

Eileen McAvoy Boylen is a freelance writer and a frequent contributor to *The Boston Globe*. She received a Master of Communications and an MBA from Boston University. She works as a ghostwriter and also runs a successful communications consulting business writing Web copy, marketing materials and e-newsletters for companies in the Boston Area. She lives with her husband, George, in Hull, Massachusetts.

About the Publisher

The Crossroad Publishing Company publishes CROSSROAD and HERDER & HERDER books. We offer a 200-year global family tradition of books on spiritual living and religious thought. We promote reading as a time-tested discipline for focus and understanding. We help authors shape, clarify, write, and effectively promote their ideas. We select, edit, and distribute books. Our expertise and passion is to provide wholesome spiritual nourishment for heart, mind, and soul through the written word.

You Might Also Like

Ingo Swann

The Great Apparitions of Mary
An Examination of the Twenty-Two
Supranormal Appearances

Paperback, 249 pages, ISBN 978-08245-16147

The great apparitions of Mary, starting with Guadalupe in 1531, occur with a steady and increasing drumbeat across the decades and centuries. The places and the principals involved change, but the messages calling people to turn from lives of violence and sin and to seek repentance are remarkably similar. This fascinating and compelling account of the appearances challenges readers of every faith to reflect on the messages and their possible consequences for our civilization and our future.

Support your local bookstore or order directly from the publisher at www.CrossroadPublishing.com

To request a catalog or inquire about quantity orders, please e-mail sales@CrossroadPublishing.com

The Crossroad Publishing Company

You Might Also Like

Jim McManus

All Generations Will Call Me Blessed
Mary at the Millennium

Paperback, 192 pages, ISBN 978-08245-17878

Mary the mother of Jesus was the only person present at the three major events in the Christian history of salvation: the Incarnation, the Crucifixion, and Pentecost. In this careful consideration of the holy mother, Redemptorist Jim McManus helps us ponder the mystery and grace of her presence and being. Though rooted in Catholic theology and seen through the lens of Vatican II, *All Generations Will Call Me Blessed* offers Protestant perspectives on Mary as well.

Support your local bookstore or order directly
from the publisher at
www.CrossroadPublishing.com

To request a catalog or inquire about
quantity orders, please e-mail
sales@CrossroadPublishing.com

✝ **The Crossroad Publishing Company**